RELENTLESS

Published by SuccessBooks®, Lake Mary, FL.
SuccessBooks® is a registered trademark.

ISBN: 979-8-9951391-0-2
LCCN: 2026905778

Most SuccessBooks® titles are available at special quantity discounts for bulk purchases for sales promotions, premiums, fundraising, and educational use. Special versions or book excerpts can also be created to fit specific needs.

For more information, please write:

SuccessBooks®
3415 W. Lake Mary Blvd. #950370
Lake Mary, FL 32795
or call 1.877.261.4930

Visit us online at: www.CelebrityPressPublishing.com.

RELENTLESS

SUCCESS BOOKS®

CONTENTS

CHAPTER 1

BECOMING BIONIC

BY LISA NICHOLS

You could practically see the heat rising from the asphalt as forty girls crowded around the chalk-drawn starting line.

Sweat gathered at the base of my neck, but I was unbothered. My mind could focus only on a single thought: *This might be the day I finally belong.*

You see, that moment was to be the end of shame and loneliness. Weeks prior, my life had completely changed. It was 1978, and I was part of the very first class of Black students being bussed from South Central Los Angeles into the Valley. Integration sounded noble when the adults explained it. It would mean a better education, better resources, better opportunities, and my parents had worked hard to make sure I qualified. They were excited, and their enthusiasm was contagious. I drank the Kool-Aid and got excited, too.

We were a bus full of wide-eyed kids, holding onto each other, pretending not to be scared, certain that this journey into the unknown would prove to be the start of a new and better life. As the bus pulled into my new school's lot, I expected to see smiling faces and welcome posters. Nothing could have prepared me for what we were met with instead. Parents lined the fence of the school holding signs. Not welcome signs, but *protest* signs. "Go back to where you came from." "Not our children. Not our school." Some shouted. Some sneered. A few even threw tomatoes. Where I lived, everyone looked like me, so this was the first time I had experienced that level of racism and the first time in my life I realized my skin color could make someone furious.

The school days were peppered with snide comments, swallowed tears, and painful isolation. But that day on the playground, at that chalk starting line... everything was going to change. The teachers had announced tryouts for *Charlie's Angels* and *The Bionic Woman*.

To a lonely little girl who loved running, dancing, jumping, and pretending to be a superhero, this was oxygen. This was hope. Over a hundred kids showed up to watch forty girls try out for three Angels, one Bionic Woman, and one alternate. I didn't even notice at first that I was the only Black girl trying out.

Event One: The 100-yard dash. "On your mark, get set, GO!" All 40 of us took off, and I sprinted ahead. I turned to see the other girls 50 yards behind me, and I crossed the finish line first. "Lisa Nichols wins Event One!" My heart cracked open with possibility. Event Two: A roll-stop-freeze move on hot asphalt. The other girls complained about the heat, but not me. I rolled, popped up, flipped my short afro-pigtails like they were long flowing hair, and shouted, "Freeze, sucker!" That's when I heard the judge announce, "Lisa Nichols wins Event Two!"

Hope flooded my chest. I could already picture myself sitting at my new lunch table with a new group of friends, walking down the hallway with a group of friends instead of slinking through it alone. I just had to get through the third event, and then my new life could finally start.

Event Three: Jumping over a chair—the Bionic Woman trial. This was a big one. There were only 8 girls left. I watched as the other girls failed to clear the chair, many of them falling flat on their faces. But I knew I could do this. I leapt, cleared that chair, and just for good measure, struck a Wonder Woman pose and added the sound effects from the Bionic Woman show. "Lisa Nichols wins Event Three!" And just like that, I could practically taste the relief of belonging. I had this in the bag. I could finally stop lying when my parents asked me how my day was. I would finally stop being teased by Brian, who told me every day that God dropped me in the tar pit or left me in the oven too long. Brian would eat his words because I was about to become a Charlie's Angel!

The judges huddled, but I knew I didn't have anything to worry about. After all, I had won every single event, so all that was left to do now was hear my name being called. The main judge stood up. "Angel #1 is... Sharon!" That was ok. There were two more spots. "Angel #2 is... Diane." A small flutter of panic made itself known in my belly, but I shoved it down. I had dominated all three events. Surely the last spot is mine. "And Angel #3 is… Sarah!" My chest tightened, but I told myself it was ok. Clearly, they saw me more as the Bionic Woman. "And the Bionic Woman is… Linda!" Linda's scream cut through the air as she ran past me to join the other girls. I was disappointed, but I held out one last hope. I could be the alternate. That was fine with me. Maybe since I was new, they thought I should be the alternate instead of a lead role. "And the alternate is…Tiffany!"

The crowd got quiet, sensing the injustice, but no one said a word. They simply filed back into the school, leaving me there, devastated and trying to understand the impossible.

I gathered my nerves, walked up to the judges and asked, "Why didn't you choose me? I won every event." They looked at each other and then came the answer that changed my relationship with myself: "Lisa, you're right," the one judge said, "You did win every event. But we can't choose you because you don't look like any of the Angels or the Bionic Woman. Try again next year…if you look more like them then."

That was the day something cracked inside me. The day my joy dimmed. The day I began to question my hair. My skin. My worth. I didn't know then that the story wasn't over. I didn't know then that this wound would become the birthplace of my relentless refusal to disappear…and that the girl left standing on that hot asphalt would one day return to that moment and rewrite it completely.

THE BIRTH OF RELENTLESSNESS

For the next ten years, I lived in a strange half-light. Smiling on the outside, performing well, achieving enough, but I never felt full joy. You see, when the world tells you, "You are not enough because of how you look," you begin to negotiate pieces of your identity. I negotiated with my hair. I negotiated with my reflection. I negotiated with my voice. I didn't know how close I was to becoming a muted version of myself. With time, however, a relentless commitment to my own unfolding took root. People think being relentless means grinding until you have nothing left. But relentlessness is not exhaustion, it is *alignment.*

To be relentless is to hold an unwavering commitment to your growth, your truth, and your identity. It is to listen to the quiet stirrings in your soul that move you in the direction you want to go. I would come to learn that relentlessness is not a quality of force, but one of *conviction*. It is a steadfast willingness to adhere to your values, even when the moment asks you to abandon them.

Relentlessness means that my beliefs are not up for public vote. My integrity does not punch out when things get inconvenient. What you repeatedly choose to stand for becomes who you are, and who you are determines what you build, what you tolerate, and what you walk away from. When identity is fragile, values become borrowed and shaped by approval, fear, or survival. But when identity is anchored, we form values that we refuse to betray. You no longer ask, *Will this make me acceptable?* You ask, *Is this aligned?* That is how we break barriers for ourselves and others; not from becoming more palatable, but from becoming more *whole*.

THE OPRAH SHOW SMACKDOWN

It was 2007, and I had just been invited to appear on *The Oprah Winfrey Show*. Oprah was my grandmother's favorite talk show host, so I knew I had to take her to Chicago with me. The girl who had picked cotton at age 10 was going to set off on the grand adventure of accompanying me to the Oprah Winfrey set! She was so proud. For years, she had watched the show and noticed in the credits that guests of the Oprah Winfrey show stayed at the Omni Hotel. She told everyone we encountered that we were staying at the Omni Hotel, "where guests of the Oprah Winfrey Show stay!"

The next morning, Harpo Studios sent a limo to pick us up. My grandmother, wrapped in cream chinchilla, looked like royalty. I put on my Louboutin pumps and my coat and was just about to escort her out the door when her expression suddenly changed from one of joy to one of disapproval. "Lisa," she said sternly, "Go make your bed." I blinked, sort of confused, but this was Grandma, and it didn't matter how old I was, I obeyed Grandma. I took off my shoes, took off my coat, and walked back to the bedroom to make my bed. I returned and said, "Ok, Grandma, time to go." I put everything back on and started walking toward the door. But Grandma stood still. "Now," she said, "Go and clean out the sink basin." Now I'm getting nervous. I don't understand what's going on here, and I don't want the Harpo limo to leave without us! I take off my shoes and coat again and go to the bathroom to clean out the sink basin. That's when I hear my grandma yell, "And clean out BOTH of them!" I do as I am told and make my way cautiously back to the foyer to try to leave the hotel for the third time. She stopped me again. "And leave the housekeeper a tip," she said, adding a bit forcefully, "a *good* one." I finally asked, "Grandma… what is going on?"

She stood up tall, graceful, and strong and said, "Your great-grandmother was a housekeeper. When people knew she was coming, they left their homes extra nasty. You won't do that today. And when your great grandma got a tip, we had meat that night." The lesson finally started to sink in. Then she delivered the truth that would become the bedrock of my leadership style and the lens through which I now filter every move I make. "You're not walking in those fancy shoes on carpet," she said. "You're walking on the shoulders of your ancestors. Everyone that came before you made this possible for you. And you *will* do right by us." I finally got it.

The highlight of that day was not Oprah Winfrey. It was Grandma. What I learned was that values cannot be seasonal. Integrity is not always convenient. In fact, my grandmother often said that your conviction and your convenience don't live on the same block! In that moment, I learned that relentlessness isn't about rising above others. It's about carrying your people with you, honoring their labor, and refusing to forget where you came from.

Grandma showed me that success without reverence is hollow, and that a relentless life is one built in gratitude, dignity, and respect for every shoulder that lifted you. I walked into Harpo Studios that day dressed for television, but I walked out dressed in a new sense of conviction, ready to lead with honor wherever my feet would land next.

WHO YOU BECOME WHEN YOU REFUSE TO BREAK

When I think back on my journey, there were certainly moments that required extraordinary strength, grit, and toughness. But I never let those moments turn me to stone. Being relentless does not mean becoming armored, sharp, or closed. True relentlessness is *wholeness.*

It is the decision to remain human in a world that rewards disconnection. To forgive what feels unforgivable. To love what the world has labeled unlovable, including the parts of yourself you were taught to negotiate, hide, or abandon. Relentless humanity does not deny pain or pretend it didn't hurt. It simply refuses to let pain become the place where the heart shuts down. A relentless spirit is strong without becoming cold, soft without becoming fragile. This is where identity is forged; not in what you endure, but in how you choose to remain intact while enduring it. Relentlessness means I do not let history dictate my future. And I do not bargain my values away for approval.

My grandmother was right: conviction and convenience don't live on the same block. To be relentless means to choose conviction, every time. And sometimes, when you choose it long enough, life brings you back to the very place where it once tried to take something from you, this time to *return* it.

I was 23 years old when I found myself standing on stage in front of 6,000 people in a Baptist church in Los Angeles, performing a rich, powerful poem I had written called *At the End of My Block*. When I finished, the entire church rose to its feet. As I walked down the aisle, elders laid hands on me. Mothers hugged me. Strangers spoke life over me. And then I heard a voice behind me. "You were amazing." I turned, and my breath caught.

There before me, standing three feet away, was Lindsay Wagner. The Bionic Woman herself. I burst into tears. "I wanted to be you," I sobbed. "And they wouldn't let me. I won every race. I jumped the highest. I did everything right, and they still didn't choose me." Lindsay placed her hands on my shoulders and said gently, "Lisa, I'm just an actress. But based on your story and what I heard today, *you* are the real Bionic Woman."

Sometimes healing arrives through recognition and long-awaited redemption. Somewhere in your life, there is a chalk line that you weren't allowed to cross. A path you were barred from. A room you were locked out of. Relentlessness is what you choose next. It is the stubborn refusal to shrink or quit. It is honoring the shoulders you stand on, protecting your humanity in a world that profits from its erosion, and choosing alignment over acceptance again and again.

When you live that way—rooted in values, faithful to your identity, committed to staying whole—you do not need to chase destiny. It reveals itself. And one day, often when you least expect it, life will circle back and return what was once denied; not because you became more palatable, but because you became more *you*.

When you refuse to disappear, perseverance becomes authorship. And you don't just *survive* a series of moments; you rewrite the meaning of them, until one by one you understand their vital role in your becoming.

About Lisa

Lisa Nichols is one of the world's most-requested speakers, as well as a media personality and corporate CEO, whose global platform reaches over 170 countries and serves over 80 million people. Lisa's social media reach is over 2.4 million followers.

As Founder and Chief Executive Officer of Motivating the Masses, Inc., Lisa has helped develop workshops and programs that have transformed thousands of businesses, and the lives of entrepreneurs. As a result of her training, her students become unforgettable speakers, best-selling authors, and 6 and 7-figure entrepreneurs.

Lisa's extraordinary story of transforming her own life from public assistance to leading a multi-million-dollar enterprise is the inspiration behind her bold mission to teach others that it is possible to do the same. Today, fans worldwide revere Lisa for her mastery of teaching people how to accomplish unfathomable goals and tap into their limitless potential.

CHAPTER 2

WHEN DEATH TAUGHT ME TO LIVE: FROM CAREGIVER TO CEO

BY DEMETRA DIMOKOPOULOS

The fluorescent lights of the cancer ward had become my sunrise and sunset. For thirty consecutive days, I'd watched them flicker to life, marking another twelve-hour shift in a plastic chair beside my grandfather's hospital bed. The smell of antiseptic lingered, and the rhythmic beeping of monitors had become my soundtrack. Around me, other families held their own vigils. Some ended with tearful goodbyes. Each time a bed emptied, I gripped my grandfather's hand tighter, as if my determination alone could anchor him to this world.

I was twenty-nine, supposedly building my legal and business career, yet here I sat, with power-of-attorney documents spread across my lap, GMAT prep books abandoned in my house, my entire life on hold. The doctors spoke in percentages and probabilities, but I heard only one message: time was running out. Not just his time, but mine too. Because in that sterile room, surrounded by the dying, one question consumed me: If I died tomorrow, would I be proud of how I lived?

The answer terrified me more than death itself.

THE PERFECT STORM

I hadn't planned to become my grandfather's caregiver so quickly. Everything seemed to change overnight in terms of his care needs. I'd been meticulously reviewing patent applications, attending networking events, and secretly studying for the GMAT at dawn. My MBA dream felt tangible then, a ladder to climb out of the predictability of legal support work. I'd already spent years in roles that felt like expensive suits that never quite fit—professional, respectable, but fundamentally misaligned with who I was becoming.

Then came the diagnosis. Terminal. The word landed like a Supreme Court ruling, final and beyond appeal. My Greek family erupted in the chaos that tragedy brings—tears, shouting, prayer candles, and casseroles. But when the dust settled, everyone looked to me. The responsible one. The one with legal training. The one without children or a husband to consider. He appointed me as his power of attorney to act when my mom couldn't. We were basically taking turns in the role to cover a twenty-four-hour period each day.

I cleared my calendar, paused my GMAT studies, and moved into the rhythm of hospitals—morning rounds, afternoon procedures, evening vigils. I learned to decode medical jargon and advocate fiercely when exhausted nurses missed his pain. I became an expert in the business of dying, though no one puts that on a résumé.

The hardest part wasn't the logistics. It was sitting alone by his bedside, consumed by the sounds that tormented me and the fear of the unknown. He slept most of the day while holding my left hand. I spent my time fearing the stages of decline I'd read about in the pamphlet the hospital gave to me, preparing me for his death.

WHEN EVERYTHING COLLAPSED

He died on a Tuesday morning. I moved through the day feeling numb, making funeral arrangements and emphasizing the importance of his haircut to the funeral director. This seemingly minor detail should not be overlooked for a lifelong barber. I returned home to isolate myself from the excitement and New Year's Eve fervor felt throughout the city. I spent Saturday at his funeral, numb in a black dress, accepting condolences in two languages while my mind felt wrapped in cotton.

I returned to work the following Monday, hoping routine would restore some normalcy. My desk looked exactly as I'd left it, and the fluorescent lights in the office now reminded me of the hospital. I moved through each day in a daze, surrounded by whispers and media reports speculating on the waves of departures at our firm. My mind spun as I digested each news article and absorbed the tension around me. Then came the news I'd feared.

Heenan Blaikie, the law firm where I worked, was shutting down. I first learned this information the way the rest of the nation did when it was announced on the 6 p.m. news. Then I saw the company's internal announcement.

The closure didn't affect just our office, but the entire national operation. A forty-one-year-old institution with more than 500 lawyers. The news outlets called it "unprecedented" and "shocking." I sat on my couch, while grief and unemployment collided in my chest like tectonic plates.

My phone buzzed. Then buzzed again. And again. "Have you seen the news?" "Are you okay?" "What are you going to do?"

I spent the rest of February in a ball of nerves as I navigated frantic calls from clients worried about their files, media calls, and job interview requests, all while packing up files in boxes. I was eager to receive my termination package that would shed some light on my immediate future.

Everyone would have understood if I'd given up then. If I'd crawled into bed and let the weight of loss, both personal and professional, bury me.

Instead, I did something that still surprises me: I went to the QS World MBA Tour.

THE RELENTLESS PIVOT

The Hilton conference rooms buzzed with ambition—hundreds of hopeful applicants clutching folders, practicing elevator pitches, wearing their best interview suits. I showed up in the only blazer that still fit after a month of hospital vending machine meals, carrying brochures I could barely focus on reading. I wasn't there to apply. I just needed to stay connected to the dream, to remember there was something beyond grief and unemployment.

But sometimes the universe has different plans. I found myself in impromptu interviews with European schools. One admissions director, perhaps seeing something desperate and determined in my eyes, mentioned their application deadline was still weeks away. "The GMAT score can come later," he said.

I applied to one school, Copenhagen Business School. While adapting to my new role during the day and editing Supreme Court submissions, I crafted my CBS application at night, pouring my fractured story into mini-essays on leadership and resilience. I wrote about transformation while still drowning in my own. The acceptance came faster than expected, conditional upon achieving a specific GMAT score.

First attempt: failed. The grief fog was too thick, my anxiety too loud. The test center felt like another hospital room—fluorescent lights, institutional chairs, the weight of someone else determining my fate. The environmental similarities triggered my anxiety and overwhelm.

I refused to accept it. For six weeks, I restructured my entire existence around that test. Wake at 3 a.m. Study until 7 a.m. Full workday at the firm. Sleep by 9 p.m. Repeat. I turned myself into a machine because feeling like a machine was better than feeling the grief. Some friends thought I'd lost my mind. Maybe I had. But madness and determination can look surprisingly similar when you're desperate enough.

Second attempt: I sat in that testing chair, shaking as the computer calculated my score. When the numbers appeared, above what I needed, I nearly collapsed. Not from joy, but from exhaustion. From relief. From the strange sensation of a door opening against all odds. I was very lucky that this was my situation. Not all of my peers fared as well.

BREAKING EVERY RULE

Moving to Denmark meant breaking every unspoken rule of my Greek upbringing. Good Greek daughters don't move across the world alone. They don't prioritize career over family. They certainly don't leave the country while still grieving, unmarried, approaching thirty.

At the Greek consulate, people in the waiting area asked repeatedly if I was meeting a boyfriend in Denmark. When I said "no," I was met with confused looks and even suspicion, as if a woman choosing education over romance was inherently fraudulent. Relatives whispered about my "delayed" life—no husband, no children, now fleeing to Scandinavia like some kind of modern exile.

But Denmark represented something I desperately needed: distance from the ghosts. A country where equality wasn't a debate but an assumption. Where my worth wouldn't be measured in my proximity to traditional milestones but in my capacity to rebuild and contribute.

The MBA year passed in a blur of strategic frameworks and leadership theories, but underneath, I was reassembling myself. Every group project, every presentation, every late-night study session was a small act of defiance against the grief that wanted to swallow me whole. I secured a job on my first day, writing business cases about Danish startups, and threw myself into the startup incubator at the Copenhagen School of Entrepreneurship.

It was there, surrounded by people building something from nothing, that I finally understood my grandfather's last gift. That month in the hospital hadn't just taught me about death; it had taught me about the urgency of living. Every flatline I'd witnessed, every family I'd seen shattered, had asked the same question: What are you waiting for?

THE BIRTH OF DEMI DEE

Returning to Canada after my MBA, I faced a choice: return to the safety of legal work or build something entirely my own. The responsible choice was obvious. The safe choice was clear. Instead, I chose entrepreneurship. I chose entrepreneurship while still working a full-time job in the legal sector. I have been bootstrapping this business ever since, in a very slow, painful progression as I navigate the ups and downs of entrepreneurship.

But imposter syndrome hit immediately. Who was I to call myself CEO? To claim expertise? To take up space in rooms full of "real" entrepreneurs? So I created Demi Dee, an alter ego who could do everything Demetra couldn't. Demi could pitch without shaking. Demi could post on social media without cringing. Demi could claim her worth without apology.

What started as a coping mechanism became a bridge. Every time I introduced myself as Demi, I stepped closer to becoming her. Every networking event I forced myself to attend, every pitch competition I entered despite the terror, every "no" I collected like twisted trophies. They all served the transformation.

Today, I run an online health coaching business focused on mothers of tween daughters. I help women break generational patterns around body image and self-worth—the very patterns that once told me my value was tied to traditional milestones I kept missing. The business wasn't an overnight success. Most nights, I wanted to quit. Some nights, I did quit—only to wake at 3 a.m. (old habits die hard) and try again.

The skeptics were vocal. Why wasn't I profitable yet? Why was it taking so long? Why not remain on the legal career path and become a lawyer? But I'd learned something vital in that cancer ward: the people who judge your journey are rarely the ones who've walked a similar path. True entrepreneurs never questioned my timeline. They knew. They understood that building something meaningful while healing from trauma isn't a sprint. It's the ultimate endurance test.

THE INTEGRATION

That girl who wrote her first book at twenty-one, documenting an environmental tragedy that devastated a community, was practicing for this moment. The woman who held her grandfather's hand through thirty days of dying was learning that time is not guaranteed. The professional who lost everything—her family member, her job, her sense of identity—she was discovering that rock bottom can become a foundation.

Every version of me—the caregiver, the griever, the unemployed professional, the international student, the struggling entrepreneur—they weren't separate stories. They were one story of relentless becoming. Of refusing to let circumstances write my ending. Understanding the gap between who I was and who I wanted to be wasn't talent or timing. It was tenacity.

My business now helps women navigate their own transformations. When clients tell me it's too late, they're too old, too stuck, too anything, I share my story. Not the polished version, but the real one—the 3 a.m. study sessions through grief fog, the failed GMAT attempt, the years of bootstrap entrepreneurship that nearly broke me. Because they need to know that relentlessness isn't pretty. It's not Instagram-worthy. It's messy, exhausting, and sometimes irrational.

But it's also the only force powerful enough to transform tragedy into triumph.

THE CALL FORWARD

If you're reading this from your own hospital chair, literal or metaphorical, know this: Your current circumstances are not your final chapter. That question that haunts you at 3 a.m., about whether you're living the life you actually want? That's not anxiety. That's your soul demanding more.

The path forward won't look like anyone else's. It might require you to break family traditions, disappoint people who love you, or create an alter ego just to survive your own becoming. You might fail the test, literally or figuratively. You might lose everything that feels stable just as you're reaching for something greater.

But here's what those thirty days in the cancer ward taught me: We're all dying. The only question is whether we'll live first. Your relatives will whisper. Your bank account will scream. Your imposter syndrome will compose entire operas of doubt. Still, you must begin. Still, you must continue. Still, you must refuse to let fear write your ending.

That vision burning in your chest? The one that feels impossible, impractical, too late to pursue? That's not delusion. That's direction. Let it be your compass when the fog rolls in. Let it pull you forward when grief, fear, or tradition try to pull you back.

Your next decision can change everything. Be relentless.

About Demetra

Demetra Dimokopoulos—known to her community as Demi Dee—is the visionary founder and CEO of The Knockout Room®. Demi is driven by a fierce commitment to dismantling barriers, redefining beauty standards, and crafting an immersive world at the intersection of wellness, storytelling, and social change, where women and girls thrive. What began as a bold wellness space for working moms and their tween daughters has blossomed into a vibrant ecosystem where programs, rituals, and community converge to ignite generational transformation.

Demi's work is practical, playful, and fiercely human. She designs gamified wellness programs that go beyond exercise to address the emotional and psychological hurdles that keep women stuck in cycles of guilt, burnout, and self-neglect. Her signature frameworks blend nutrition, movement, emotional coaching, and short repeatable rituals so that busy families can build habits that stick, model healthy boundaries, and reframe beauty and strength for the next generation.

Demi meets women where they are and offers simple, repeatable practices that make showing up for yourself possible. She coaches with warmth, humor, and blunt honesty, celebrating imperfect progress and calling boundary-setting what it is: a form of liberation.

Her approach is shaped by training and lived experience. She completed her undergraduate degree at the University of Toronto, with a double major in psychology and professional writing & communication, and her Master of Business Administration at Copenhagen, Business School with a focus on entrepreneurship, leadership, and sustainability. She is also a graduate of the Institute for Woman-Centered Coaching, Training and Leadership; a Health Coach Alliance Registered Health Coach; and a canfitpro-certified fitness professional.

Outside of program work, Demi is an extroverted introvert who treasures solitude and small rituals. She enjoys kickboxing, cycling, and rebound fitness. Her passion for language and the arts has led her to explore six languages with varying degrees of fluency, and she continues to nurture her creative spirit through writing and strumming her acoustic guitar. Demi also loves baking, binge-watching The Handmaid's Tale, and wandering in nature.

Learn more at: TheKnockoutRoom.com

CHAPTER 3

WHEN LOSING EVERYTHING LED TO FINDING MYSELF

BY GINA VAN DER VLIET

The California sun seemed to mock me as I walked down Santa Monica Boulevard. The giant Ferris wheel was spinning cheerfully on the pier while my entire world collapsed. My employer had just fired me in front of a client. He intended his cowardly theatrical performance to save his business relationship after he'd overslept for their meeting and conveniently blamed it on me. "There's a restaurant downstairs," he'd said casually after she left. "Work there for a while, and I'll hire you back."

But we both knew it didn't work that way. He was sponsoring my green card. Without his company, I'd lose my legal status in America. Nine years ago, I'd left the Netherlands as a twenty-year-old au pair with nothing but determination and a childhood dream. After fighting all that time to stay in this country, was this the end?

"Oh my god," I thought, staring at the Pacific Ocean. "This is it. My dreams have just come to a crashing halt."

As a child, watching *West Side Story* on a small television in the Netherlands, something clicked inside me so powerfully it felt like remembering rather than discovering. "I'm going to live there," I announced to my family. They laughed. My grandmother would later warn me that young girls like me ended up in prostitution in dangerous American cities. Even Katherine, a seventy-something New Yorker living in Amsterdam, summoned me to her house before I left to warn me about the perils waiting in New York City.

But at twenty, I didn't care about their fears. I applied to be an au pair through the Au Pair Homestay USA program. The application specifically stated that you couldn't request a location and that you needed a driver's license. I had neither the license nor any intention of ending up anywhere but New York. With quiet determination, I wrote "NEW YORK CITY" on the form anyway.

The universe has a sense of humor. Because I didn't have a driver's license, no suburban family would take me. I ended up exactly where I wanted to be, in Manhattan, living with Anne and her family. Anne became more than a host mother; she was a mentor and a beacon of stability. Thirty-five years later, we're still close friends. She taught me how to navigate American life with quiet confidence instead of the drama I'd grown up with in my conflict-ridden family.

After my au pair year, I was convinced more than ever that America was where I belonged. I applied for a student visa and enrolled at Hunter College, majoring in media communications with a minor in English. My mother, a teacher herself and someone who loved to control through financial support, offered to send money. I was so determined to prove I could make it on my own that when she sent a thousand dollars anyway, I sent it straight back, infuriating my mom after both banks had taken their transfer fees. "Even if I have to eat peanut butter sandwiches for a year," I told her, "I'm doing this on my own."

She never tried again. And I always landed on my feet.

Billboard Magazine hired me straight out of college. When they opened a position in Los Angeles, I became their editorial assistant, living my journalism dreams. I even got to interview Carol Decker from T'Pau. She was my teenage idol with whom I'd exchanged letters when I was seventeen, dreaming of running away to become a roadie for her band. Now I was writing a front-page story about her, feeling the incredible power that comes when women support each other across continents and years.

But Billboard wouldn't sponsor my green card. "If we do it for you, we'll have to do it for everyone," they said. "It's too complicated." My entire life hung in the balance on those words. A friend connected me with the entertainment manager who would eventually fire me on that sunny California morning in 1999. He'd promised to sponsor me, to get me involved in screenplay development. Instead, I became his secretary, and when I pushed for more creative work, he eliminated me to save face with a client. I do, however, remain grateful to him to this day—both for the initial sponsorship and for making me stronger through his duplicity.

Walking back from the Santa Monica Pier that day, devastated, I had no idea that a letter would soon make its way to my temporary address in the Netherlands. I'd entered the Diversity Visa Program—the green card lottery that was established by the Immigration Act of 1990—every year for a decade. Never winning, always hoping.

A few weeks after returning to my mother's house in defeat, the letter arrived. I'd won.

The irony wasn't lost on me. The worst thing that had happened—getting fired, losing my sponsorship—freed me from several more years of working for someone who didn't value me. Sometimes the door that slams shut is the one that needs to close.

I returned to the USA in early 2000 with a green card and genuine freedom. I bought an apartment in Harlem, NYC, with some family help and continued working in magazines—fitness and entertainment, writing about *NSYNC and Britney Spears for tween magazine M (Music, Movies and More). But after 9/11, something shifted. The fan mail from young readers was so poorly written that it broke my heart. These nine and ten-year-old girls deserved better. The subway ads for New York City Teaching Fellows started calling to me: "You remember your first-grade teacher's name. Who will remember yours?"

In 2005, despite swearing I'd never follow in my mother's footsteps, I joined the Teaching Fellows program. They needed people from other professions to teach in the hardest-to-staff schools. That's how I ended up in the Bronx, a thirty-six-year-old career changer facing parents who looked at young, lighter-skinned teachers with suspicion. "Who are these people coming into our schools thinking they know better?"

The other teachers warned me about parents who'd waited outside to confront teachers, who could be verbally aggressive when upset. I was nervous and intimidated. My mentor in the Fellows program gave me advice that changed everything: “Focus on what you fear most, then work on that.”

So I focused on the parents. Instead of avoiding them, as many colleagues did, I started reaching out. I called with good news, not just problems. “Your son did something wonderful today,” I’d say, watching their defensive walls crumble. I’d tell them directly: “You want what’s best for your child. I want what’s best for your child. We’re on the same team. How can we support each other?”

One mother worried constantly about her son’s heart condition. After school one day, as we talked about his health and his constant bouncing around despite his condition, she suddenly threw her arms around me and sobbed on my shoulder. Her tough exterior melted into vulnerability and trust. Another mother, from the Dominican Republic, confided that she wanted to become a teacher but worried her English wasn’t good enough. “Your English is great,” I told her. “We need Spanish-speaking teachers. You have exactly what it takes.” I showed her where to apply and what courses to take. I still wonder if she made it.

By my second year, I had forged some of the strongest parent relationships in the school. The partnership I’d been so afraid to forge became my greatest strength.

But it was in 2017, back in the Netherlands, when I faced my biggest fear. I returned in 2011 when my mother was diagnosed with breast cancer, giving up my coveted green card after nearly twenty-two years in the US—something I never thought I’d do. At thirty-six, I’d finally come out to myself as a lesbian, ending relationships with men that had never felt right. At thirty-eight, I’d come out to my family and friends. Now I was teaching fourth grade at an international school, newly dating my now-wife, but still closeted at work.

That morning, I walked into my classroom to find students huddled around a graphic novel, giggling and saying “Eww, they’re gay!” about two boys playing Romeo and Juliet. My heart hammered in my chest. I thought about an NYC au pair family I knew in the early nineties, how the mother had been worried to discover her son’s kindergarten teacher was gay, asking that he be moved to another class.

But these were my students making those sounds of disgust. My responsibility.

I closed the door. "Everyone, have a seat." My hands shook as I pulled up a photo on my computer and projected it on the screen—my girlfriend and me, smiling, clearly together. "You've been asking about my personal life," I said into the silence. "This is my partner. She's a woman."

You could hear a pin drop. Then one girl from Nigeria said, "Miss Gina, in my country, this isn't allowed. It's against the law." What followed was the most beautiful, open-hearted conversation I've ever witnessed. We talked about how you can't always control who you love, how laws don't always reflect what's right, and how love that doesn't hurt anyone shouldn't be feared. I encouraged them to ask me questions, and many did, eager to learn and surprised to find out gay couples are just regular people.

A sweet, naive boy looked at the photo and asked, "Does your girlfriend know you're gay?" I smiled through tears. "Well, honey, I think by now she does."

I sent messages to all the parents that afternoon, bracing for backlash. Nothing came. No complaints, no requests for transfers, no change in their warm greetings. Now, I consciously come out to each new class at the start of the year, showing my wedding photos in my PowerPoint introduction. I've never had a negative response. Not once.

Some gay teachers still risk being fired just for being themselves. In places like Texas, it's still legal to be let go of your job for being openly gay. People fear we have some magic wand that will turn their children gay, as if that's the worst thing that could happen in a world full of actual violence and hatred. But I know my visibility matters. If my students only know gay people from pride parades, all leather and flash, they miss the reality: we're teachers and accountants and parents, living ordinary lives with extraordinary love.

Teaching for twenty years has given me perspective, but it's also shown me I need more. Now I work three days a week—Wednesday through Friday—despite my family's horror- and fear-ridden stories about pension and financial security. On Tuesdays, I run my voice acting business, "Gina's Voice," finally returning to the creativity I craved since those teenage dreams of joining the Brat Pack. I'm writing my own story, the book I'll publish next year, because late bloomers need to know it's never actually too late.

The universe has always been kind to me, even when it seemed cruel. Just this week, I needed to complete a voice acting job, but I worried it would conflict with my teaching schedule. The script arrived Monday night—just in time for my Gina's Voice day. These small mercies remind me I'm supported, even when the path seems impossible.

My mentors—Lisa Nichols, Siri Lindley, Rebekah Keat, Mary Morrissey, Marci Shimoff, Tony Robbins, and Joseph McClendon III, to name a few—have taught me to control my thoughts, to catch myself in fear mode, and choose differently. Siri's voice echoes in my head during daily 5 a.m. workouts: "Yes, you can. Don't stop." She's right. We're wired for survival, which means we're wired for fear. But we can rewire ourselves for possibility.

People have underestimated me my entire life. They laughed when a nine-year-old Dutch girl said she'd live in New York. They said I wasn't responsible enough to make it as an au pair, that I would never survive without my mother's money, and never recover from losing my sponsorship. My principal in the Bronx told me I wasn't tough enough. When I returned to the Netherlands, they said the job market was terrible, and I'd never find work.

They're still saying things. I read a quote that said, "If you're not successful [yet], they say you're not good enough. If you succeed, they say you're lucky. They'll say what they want to say."

Here's what I've learned: Don't try to convince anyone else. Convince yourself. Because once *you* believe it, it happens. The gap between where you are and where you want to be isn't talent or timing or luck, but instead tenacity. It's refusing to let setbacks write your ending.

My coach recently told me something that cuts straight to the truth: "It's better to lose people who don't understand you, love you, or support you than to lose yourself." Some people won't come along on your journey. Some will hold you back, fearing your growth highlights their stagnation. Maybe you'll part ways. Maybe that's exactly what needs to happen.

Your story isn't over until you decide it is. Every closed door, every rejection, every moment that feels like failure—they're not endings. They're redirections. That firing in Los Angeles led to my green card. Coming out to my students deepened my purpose as an educator. Giving up my American dream to care for my mother led me to my wife and to finding my voice in new ways.

Relentlessness isn't about never falling. It's about always getting up, even when getting up means walking away from everything you thought you wanted. It's about sending the money back, projecting your truth on the screen, and partnering with people who frighten you. It's about believing the universe is conspiring for you, especially when evidence suggests otherwise.

Listen to yourself. Trust the pull that makes no sense to anyone else. That nine-year-old watching *West Side Story* knew something everyone else missed—that home isn't always where you're from, but where you're brave enough to go.

Be relentless about your becoming. Your next decision can change everything.

About Gina

Gina van der Vliet is a former entertainment journalist whose bylines have appeared in renowned publications such as *Billboard Magazine, The Los Angeles Daily News*, and *M* (Music, Movies and More). Driven by a lifelong passion for publishing and storytelling, Gina transitioned to education and has spent over twenty years teaching-primary school children (K–5th grade) in both the United States and the Netherlands. She is dedicated to nurturing the unique talents of her students and is a strong advocate for the power of a Growth Mindset, which she incorporates into her teaching practice.

In 2023, Gina founded Gina's Voice, a creative platform that allows her to explore voice acting, podcasting, and writing. Inspired by thought leaders including Lisa Nichols, Maya Angelou, Oprah, Marci Shimoff, and Siri Lindley, Gina is committed to helping others live their happiest and most fulfilled lives.

Beyond her professional pursuits, Gina is passionate about supporting LGBTQ+ and human rights organisations. She enjoys spending quality time with her wife, Virginie, as well as with friends, family, and in nature. Her hobbies include practising yoga, playing the ukulele, and making memories with her grandnieces, Milou and Fien.

To learn more about Gina's creative journey and projects, visit Ginasvoice.com.

CHAPTER 4

RECLAIMING TRUTH: WHEN BETRAYAL BECAME MY BREAKING POINT AND MY BREAKTHROUGH

BY CHERYLANN PROVIDENCE

The hospital discharge papers felt like sandpaper in my hands. Ectopic pregnancy. Surgery. Recovery ahead. I should have been focused on healing my body. My mind kept circling back to the phone call I'd received just days before—the one that shattered everything I thought I knew about my life.

"Your husband is married to another woman in Trinidad."

I read the words on the discharge instructions, but all I could see was that sentence playing on repeat. Third marriage. Third failure. The voices started immediately—my family, my friends, the chorus of concern that sounded more like a funeral dirge than support.

"You'll never recover from this."

"How could you not have known?"

"Maybe you're the problem."

Recovering at home, still tender from surgery, I had two choices. I could believe them. I could let this betrayal write the final chapter of my story. Or I could refuse.

I refused.

THE PATTERN I COULDN'T SEE

Looking back now, I can trace the invisible thread that connected all my relationships, all my choices, all the moments where I gave my power away. Growing up, I was the daughter who was never quite enough. My mother and siblings made it clear. I wasn't as smart as my younger brother. That message burrowed deep, creating a foundation of quicksand rather than stone.

When you're told you're less than, you start to believe it. And when you believe it, you accept treatment that confirms it.

My first two marriages. The relationships that followed. The patterns repeated like a song I couldn't stop humming, even when I hated the melody. I attracted people who sensed my uncertainty, my desperate need to prove I was worthy of love. They took advantage of that hunger.

But that third betrayal, discovering my husband had another wife, was different. Not because it hurt more, though it did. Because it happened when I was already broken open, vulnerable from surgery, stripped of the armor I usually wore.

I was the problem. Not because I deserved betrayal, but because I had built my entire life on seeking validation outside myself. From my family, men, and anyone who might confirm that I mattered.

The house I'd built without a foundation was crumbling.

THE VOICE THAT WOULDN'T QUIT

The weeks after were a blur of well-meaning advice and pitying looks. Everyone had an opinion about what I should do, who I should be, and how I should recover. The noise was deafening.

But underneath it all, there was another sound. Quieter. Steadier. Insistent.

My intuition.

Whispering warnings of red flags nudged me toward the truth I wasn't ready to face. Now, with nothing left to lose, I finally started listening.

The voice said: Rebuild.

Not just your life. Rebuild *you.*

I started small. A podcast here. A YouTube video there. I devoured content from people who had been through hell and walked out the other side holding fire. Not the polished, perfect success stories, but the messy, real, still-healing-but-moving-forward stories. The ones that didn't pretend the journey was easy, quick, or glamorous.

I listened to Oprah talk about becoming who you're meant to be. I watched Brené Brown explain vulnerability and shame. I found teachers who said the words I desperately needed to hear: What happened to you does not define you. Someone took advantage of your wounds. That's about them, not about you.

Every morning, I made a choice. Get up. Keep going. Listen to the voice.

Every morning, I also felt fear. Paralyzing, throat-closing, what-if-I-fail-again fear. The judgment hadn't stopped. If anything, it had intensified. A third divorce. At my age. With my history. The whispers followed me everywhere.

But I kept going anyway.

LEARNING TO TRUST THE WHISPER

The irony wasn't lost on me. I had spent my entire life not trusting myself, and now I was being asked to trust myself completely. To believe that the intuition I'd ignored for decades might actually know the way forward.

It started with small tests. The voice would say, "Go back to school."

Logic said I was too old, too damaged, too behind. But I enrolled anyway.

The voice said, "You're here to serve."

Fear said I had nothing to offer. But I started my coaching practice anyway.

Again and again, when I followed the whisper instead of the shoulds, things worked. Not perfectly. Not easily. But they worked. Doors that I thought were welded shut opened. Opportunities appeared that I'd convinced myself I didn't deserve.

My siblings thought I was crazy. The girl they'd written off as "not as smart" was pursuing a PhD. The same hunger for learning that had been dismissed in childhood became my superpower. I wanted to understand myself, human behavior, and what makes us choose what we choose. I needed to comprehend how I'd ended up here so I could find the map out.

Out of my three siblings, I became the only one with a doctorate. Not because I was smarter, but because I was relentless.

But the degree was just paper. The real education was happening in the 2 a.m. moments when I wanted to quit. When the voice said *keep going* and everything else said *stop*. When I had to choose between the comfort of my old patterns and the terrifying uncertainty of transformation.

I chose transformation. Again and again and again.

BUILDING ON SOLID GROUND

Here's what nobody tells you about rebuilding: you can't construct anything lasting until you understand what the foundation is made of. And for most of us, we're spiritual beings who have forgotten how to access our own power.

We turn to social media for validation. We look to relationships to complete us. We chase external markers of success, thinking they'll fill the void inside. We build and build and build on sand, then wonder why everything keeps falling apart.

I had to go deeper, not to some mystical, out-of-reach place, but to the truth that had been buried under layers of other people's expectations and judgments. I had to remember that I was whole before anyone told me I was broken. That my worth existed before anyone questioned it. That my intuition knew things my logical mind couldn't comprehend.

This became the foundation I now help my clients build. Because I've been there—on my knees, convinced my story was over. I know what it feels like to believe you're too damaged, too old, too far gone.

I know you're not.

THE MOMENT EVERYTHING SHIFTED

The turning point wasn't dramatic. There was no lightning bolt, no sudden epiphany that made everything clear. It was quieter than that. More profound.

I was listening to a podcast about manifestation and visualization, and something clicked. I had been so focused on what I'd lost—the marriages, the years, the trust—that I'd forgotten to imagine what I could gain.

So I started visualizing, not in some woo-woo way that ignored reality, but in a practical way that acknowledged where I was while refusing to stay there. I saw myself helping others. I saw myself building a practice that transformed lives. I saw myself not just surviving but thriving.

And then, even when I didn't feel ready, I took action.

The fear was still there. The doubt still whispered that I'd fail again, that people would judge me, that I wasn't qualified to help anyone when my own life had been such a mess. But I moved anyway.

This is the secret nobody tells you: relentlessness isn't about feeling confident. It's about acting despite the feeling. It's about showing up when every cell in your body says hide. It's about taking the next step when you can't see the staircase.

WHEN THE PAST SHOWS UP IN PRESENT TENSE

Recently, I met women who had written books with Lisa. They were further ahead in their journeys, more established, more *successful* by external measures. The old voice tried to resurface: too late, missed your chance, not good enough.

But the new voice, the one I'd been training and trusting and following, said something different.

"This is your opportunity. Take the leap."

So here I am. Writing my chapter. Sharing my story. Refusing to let fear or judgment or the weight of the past determine what's possible now.

Because here's what I've learned through every failure, every betrayal, every moment I wanted to quit: doing something is always better than doing nothing at all. Imperfect action beats perfect paralysis every single time.

The women who succeed aren't the ones who never feel fear. They're the ones who feel it and move anyway. They're the ones who get knocked down and get back up. They're the ones who refuse to let one chapter, even a devastating one, become the entire book.

WHAT BETRAYAL TAUGHT ME ABOUT TRUTH

The gift hidden in that third betrayal, and yes, I can call it a gift now, was that it destroyed my illusions. Not just about my husband, but about everything. About who I thought I had to be. About what I thought I needed. About where I thought my power came from.

Living in illusion feels safe until it all comes crashing down. Then you have a choice: build another illusion or build on truth.

Truth is scarier. Truth requires you to face the parts of yourself you've been hiding. Truth demands you take responsibility, not for what was done to you, but for what you do next.

I chose truth. And truth, it turns out, is the only foundation that doesn't crack under pressure.

Now, when I work with clients who are rebuilding after their own betrayals, losses, or breaking points, I take them back to foundation work first. We don't skip ahead to the sexy stuff—the business plans, marketing strategies, external success markers. We go deep.

Because if the foundation isn't solid, everything else will eventually crumble. I know. I've rebuilt that house three times the wrong way.

THE MUSCLES YOU DON'T KNOW YOU HAVE

Here's what I want you to understand if you're standing where I once stood broken:

You have muscles you haven't used yet. Strength you don't know exists. The capacity to rebuild is built into your bones, written into your DNA, waiting for you to remember it's there.

But like any muscle, it atrophies without use. You have to work it. Train it. Push it past the point of comfort again and again until it becomes strong enough to carry you.

When I first started doing this work—on myself, then with clients—everything felt impossible. My trust muscles had atrophied. My intuition muscles were weak. My belief-in-myself muscles could barely lift the weight of getting out of bed.

But I worked them. Every day. Every choice. Every time I followed the whisper instead of the scream. Every time I took action despite fear. Every time I showed up, I wanted to hide.

And slowly, steadily, relentlessly, those muscles grew.

Now, they're strong enough to help others build theirs. That's the beautiful irony of this work—your greatest pain becomes your most powerful tool for service. The very thing that almost destroyed you becomes the bridge you build for someone else to cross.

THE RED FLAGS I CAN NOW SEE

One of the most profound shifts in my journey has been developing the ability to see red flags before I'm already drowning. When your foundation is solid, when you're connected to your intuition, when you trust yourself, you don't miss the warnings anymore.

You see the inconsistencies. You feel the misalignment. You notice when someone's words don't match their actions. You recognize patterns before they repeat.

This doesn't mean you're cynical or closed off. It means you're awake. It means you value yourself enough to pay attention. It means you've learned that ignoring your intuition always costs more than trusting it.

My clients often come to me after their own betrayals, wondering how they missed the signs. They beat themselves up for being *stupid* or *blind*. But they weren't stupid. They were disconnected—from themselves, their power, and the truth that was always there waiting to be acknowledged.

Rebuilding isn't just about recovering from what happened. It's about developing the discernment to make better choices moving forward. It's about strengthening the connection to your inner knowing so you can trust yourself to navigate whatever comes next.

THE STORY THAT ISN'T OVER

I could end this chapter by telling you everything is perfect now. That I never struggle. That the work is done, and I've arrived at some final destination of enlightenment and success.

But that would be another illusion.

The truth is, I still feel fear sometimes. I still have moments of doubt. I still hear the old voices trying to convince me I'm not enough. The difference is, I don't believe them anymore. And when they get loud, I have tools to quiet them.

Relentlessness isn't about reaching a point where the struggle ends. It's about developing the capacity to keep moving through struggle. It's about building a foundation strong enough to withstand whatever storms come. It's about remembering, again and again, that your story isn't over until you say it is.

And I'm not done writing mine.

Neither are you.

THE INVITATION

If you're reading this from the wreckage of your own betrayal, your own breaking point, your own third (or fourth, or tenth) failure—know this:

You can survive. You will not be destroyed. You can love again, laugh again, trust again.

What you've gone through is not the determining factor in what comes next. Your next decision is. The muscles you're about to build are. The foundation you choose to construct is.

Yes, it will take work. Deep, uncomfortable, sometimes excruciating work. You'll have to face truths you've been avoiding. You'll have to build strength in places that feel permanently weak. You'll have to keep showing up when every instinct says hide.

But here's what I know for absolute certain: heartbreak is not the end of your story. It's a turning point. And at every turning point, you get to choose which direction to go. I'm happily married now to a great person. I chose happiness as the end of my story.

Choose truth over illusion. Choose action over paralysis. Choose relentlessness over resignation.

The gap between where you are and where you want to be isn't insurmountable. It's not even about talent, timing, or luck. It's instead about tenacity and being willing to rebuild, one choice at a time, one day at a time, one whisper-followed at a time.

Your intuition knows the way. Your strength is waiting to be discovered. Your story is ready to be reclaimed.

Be relentless about your rebirth.

Because the world needs what you'll become on the other side of this breaking point, I'm proof of that. And soon, you will be too.

About Cherylann

Cherylann Providence is a visionary Life Transformation Facilitator whose work ignites a profound awakening in women stepping into the most powerful chapter of their lives. She leads women in midlife to reclaim their brilliance, embody their purpose, and design lives that reflect the fullness of who they were always meant to be. Through her compassionate leadership and intuitive depth, Cherylann guides women to rise with courage, align with their soul's wisdom, and create lasting change that ripples across their families, communities, and future generations.

As the founder of Providence Life Mastery LLC, her legacy is rooted in elevating women to live with intention, authenticity, and unstoppable confidence. Cherylann's work continues to inspire a global movement of women who refuse to shrink, choosing instead to rise, realign, and rediscover the extraordinary power within.

Learn more at: cherylannprovidence.com

CHAPTER 5

SOVEREIGN ALIGNMENT

BY AMIRAH ANSAAR

I was eight years old when my world shifted with one sentence. We were in the small bedroom where my mother, the woman I had always called Mom, kept folded blankets stacked like precise little clouds. She sat on the edge of the bed, called me to her, and wrapped my hands in hers.

"Biologically," she said, calm and clear, "I'm not your mom. But I love you just the same." She explained that the siblings I'd grown up with were biologically related to each other, but not to me.

Behind the ache, something clicked into place, puzzle pieces finally finding their corners. The quiet sense of being different finally had a name. Then came the question that sat heavy in my chest: If I don't belong here… then where do I belong?

That question planted a seed of wonder. Who am I now? What does this mean for me? My mother cupped my face and said again that she loved me, that I was hers by choice. That assurance landed like a stake in the ground. But the truth had entered the room, and there would be no going back.

I didn't have language for it then, but a vow was forming in me. I may never know my biological mother's why, and I honor the mother who chose me; what I did know was this: I would become the mother my soul needed, first for the little girl inside me, then for the daughter I would one day raise, and eventually for women who felt unclaimed by the places and people that were supposed to hold them. I wouldn't have called it relentless at eight. But that was the beginning.

MISALIGNMENT

After the bedroom truth, curiosity surged. I wanted more freedom and identity than I'd been given. My desire to explore was misinterpreted as discontent. I was relocated, first to therapeutic schools, then to group homes. With each new placement came new rules taped to refrigerators and new names on chore charts. Some houses hummed with constant television. I learned that people love according to their capacity, not always according to your need. I also learned to find the Great I AM (God) in the gaps.

Between moves, I prayed. Between disappointments, I cried in the mirror to my Creator. Between new last names, I promised the little girl inside me: *I will become the mother you needed.* Staff sometimes mistook my silence for agreement and my survival mode for not caring. The system translated grief into labels. Sometimes the labels squeezed; sometimes they swallowed you whole.

At seventeen, I emancipated. Not as rebellion, though the papers would make it look that way, but as stewardship. I got a job and found a small apartment. I didn't have a plan or a net, only the willingness to believe the next step would appear. Growth doesn't require readiness. It requires willingness and faith that your steps are ordered even when the path is unclear. Relentlessness is not loud. Relentlessness is a daily "yes."

THE FAMILY RECALIBRATED

On my own, I longed for family; the steady kind that didn't end because a calendar flipped or a file changed hands. I married. I became a mother. For twelve years, marriage became a classroom I never signed up for. Harm can dress itself in respectability. Childhood wounds can blur every red flag until you're standing in a storm without a coat, telling yourself rain is only water. I stayed because those wounds whispered, "At least you aren't alone. At least your child has two parents. At least..."

But "at least" is a dangerous lullaby. When my daughter reached an age where she could absorb the atmosphere, something rose in me. I began to prepare for a different life. I made folders and lists. I gathered documents and placed copies where the wrong hands could not get them. I had learned order in a world that depended on chaos. I would exit with order.

By day, I studied. Nursing first, because I have always had a healer's hands. Then computer science, because systems fascinate me: how parts become whole, how signals travel, how stability is designed. Curiosity, when honest, is relentless. That curiosity walked me into an aerospace engineering corporation, where machines have missions and instruments tell the truth even in turbulence.

My assignment there settled something in me: I built and calibrated aircraft compasses, instruments designed to return to True North despite magnetic noise. Pilots rely on those quiet needles in the middle of weather and night. I learned the difference between drift and disaster. I learned that what you recalibrate regularly, you can trust.

SYSTEMS AND SIGNALS

Sometimes, True North reveals itself in the ordinary. Years later, during a season when I was working in Marketing at Bose Corporation, a coworker named Barry kept disappearing into a back room. He walked back, wrapped in the server room's hush and steady vibration. "What's in there?" I asked. He smiled and motioned for me to follow. The door opened: towering racks, bundled cables, thousands of status lights. The room hummed with steady power. Something in me awakened. "This," I thought. "I want to understand this."

Barry handed me a book. It was an invitation. I couldn't afford a library of manuals, so I took my daughter to Barnes & Noble, found a quiet corner, and studied Microsoft certification guides like scripture, one exam at a time. Those credentials became a bridge from systems to security, from wiring and servers to threat modeling, hardening, incident response, and the disciplined art of protecting the crown jewels without breaking the people doing the work.

I had found my lane: cybersecurity with a healer's heart. The same hands that calibrated compasses to True North began calibrating teams, teaching them to reduce noise, patch vulnerabilities, practice drills, and design escalation paths you could count on at 3 a.m. The compass metaphor followed me: reduce magnetic interference, realign, move. The job wasn't to make fear our focus; it was to make order our practice.

SOVEREIGN CHOICE

There's a version of my story where the exit is spectacle: sirens, suitcases, and shouting. That is not my version. I waited for a window and, when it opened, I moved. I treated leaving a twelve-year abusive marriage like a mission-critical cutover. Inventory. Allies. Timeline. Protection. When the moment came, I packed our things, took my daughter, and left.

People imagine leaving as the end of pain; often, it is the beginning of healing, which is messier and braver. I set rituals, routines, and a home that smelled like soup and lemon. I chose what came into our space like a gatekeeper at a sanctuary. Laughter on purpose. Emotional intelligence taught out loud. We were building new air, breath by breath.

In time, I married my beloved husband, one who honors my calling, my boundaries, and even the girl I once was. My daughter grew into her own power. My two teenage grandchildren call me Yeye and reignited my life. They reminded me to design for longevity over urgency, to turn attention into affection and minutes into memories.

When my daughter became a teen mother, I kept a promise I made as a child: mother the mother. We built a scaffold (childcare, classes, rides, meals, rest) and treated love like logistics. She learned her son; I ensured life made room for them both. We didn't outrun statistics; we out-organized them. Today, the baby who slept on my chest is an amazing young adult, and the young woman I steadied now stands steady on her own. My granddaughter is thriving with T1D, and my daughter's steady, intelligent care is relentless love in motion: systems that hold, joy that stays, and faith that keeps rhythm.

ORDER AT THE TABLE

Around the time my career deepened, my kitchen turned into a classroom. Halfway through an ingredient list, I felt the same old tug: What are we ingesting? We weren't eating nourishment; we were eating experiments. Artificial sweeteners. Preservatives. Flavor enhancers wearing health halos. I began advocating for Food Safety in plain language: teaching families how to read labels and why GMO transparency matters. For me, it wasn't politics; it was dignity, choice, and informed consent. If food is bioengineered, people deserve to know. I spoke at community gatherings, answered questions in line at the market, and built simple guides. Concern became calling; calling turned into community. That work was the seed of Wellness Revolutionary.

THE VOICE THAT HEALS

Through all of it, I discovered the instrument I was born with: my voice. Not just words, but frequency, calm in a crisis, clarity in confusion, courage in the quiet. The same voice that soothed a child in the night became the one that secured stakeholders in difficult meetings. The same cadence that prayed in the car became the cadence that teaches leaders to breathe when dashboards go red.

I am a Radio Personality, which means my voice must carry truth across air and static; traffic breaks, wellness segments, calls that crackle with fatigue and hope. Radio taught me to be concise and generous; cybersecurity taught me to be precise and kind; ministry taught me to be present and brave. Over time, I realized I'm the voice of sovereign law, not legalism, but divine alignment, spoken in love. I speak to help people re-order what chaos has scrambled.

LOWER THE NOISE, RAISE THE CLARITY

There was a night in a healing circle when a woman finally said the hard thing out loud. Her hands trembled; her voice was a whisper. As the words landed, I watched faces shift, not in judgment, but in fear. You could feel the room brace. It wasn't the truth they were resisting; it was the uncertainty that truth would require. If we name this, what changes? What do we have to do to move, forgive, rebuild?

I've learned people don't resist change; they resist not knowing how to cross the threshold. I slowed the room. I asked everyone to place a hand over the heart and breathe, four in, eight out, until the room softened. Then we named what was true (no story, just facts), contained it (time limits, one voice at a time), and set three next steps: one boundary, one call for support, one ritual to steady the nervous system.

Nothing magical happened to the past, but something holy happened to the future: the room exhaled. The story didn't change; their confidence did. In aerospace, we reduce magnetic noise to trust the heading; in healing, we reduce emotional noise to trust the heart. The work is the same: lower the anxiety, raise the clarity, rehearse the move, and uncertainty becomes a doorway instead of a wall.

INPUTS BECOME IMPRINTS

As my work grew, my home stayed my first classroom. I saw that wellness isn't just food. It's inputs: what we feed body, mind, spirit, calendars, and devices. A phone can steal a child's heart by stealing a parent's attention. A calendar can starve a marriage; a notification can fray a nervous system. Every input leaves an imprint. That revelation became Wellness Revolutionary, my work of restoring sacred order in a digital age, so technology serves destiny. It also became Sacred Trust Ministries, an ecclesiastically sovereign, faith-based 508(c)(1)(a) sanctuary and ministry alliance existing to restore sacred order, advance whole-person healing, and grow moral, spiritual, and cultural leadership by strengthening families, protecting the vulnerable, and equipping communities through prayer, education, and practical care.

I trained formally. I completed the Institute for Integrative Nutrition (IIN) and earned the National Board Certified Health & Wellness Coach (NBHWC) credential to anchor my approach in science and standards. I became a Positive Intelligence® (PQ)-certified coach because if we don't weaken inner saboteurs and strengthen the Sage, no system holds. Then I distilled the practice into the Personal Technical Wellness Series™, practical pathways for households, teams, and leaders to reclaim attention, redesign routines, and implement humane tech. Audit. Align. Automate. Repeat, not as a sprint, but as a rhythm.

Attention needed its own handbook. My book series begins with *Focused: Mastering Attention in a Distracted World*, a field guide for restoring custody of your mind and building systems that protect deep work, deep rest, and deep relationships. *Focused* teaches mindset and method; the *Personal Technical Wellness Series* installs habits and tools. Attention is love, measured in minutes.

THE ALIGNMENT LOOP

People ask how I came up with my framework. The framework found me. It's what my life kept doing when it wanted to heal: Audit → Align → Automate.

Audit the chaos. Tell yourself the holy truth about beginnings and betrayals, burnout and blue light, labels and lies, about what's on your plate and in your feed. You cannot heal what you do not reveal.

Align to sacred order. Put God where God goes. Put health where health goes. Put family and purpose where they belong. Put technology where it belongs, after values are decided and boundaries are drawn. In aerospace and security, I learned the same thing: compasses drift and systems decay. Alignment isn't one-and-done; relentlessness is recalibrating to True North. Automate what protects your peace. Don't fight the same battle every day; build a gate. Calendar blocks, notification rules, zero-trust for your attention, Sabbath protocols, runbooks for crisis, rituals that make rest non-negotiable. Make it easier to choose what grows you.

The point isn't performance. The point is presence: to God, to yourself, to the people entrusted to you.

IDENTITY, ALIGNED

My name is a map: Amirah means to lead. Ansaar means to help. I lead and help. I'm wired like a compass: magnetic toward meaning, steady under pressure. Freedom calls me forward; responsibility keeps me true. My joy is simple: master my own path and light yours as I go.

If you're standing at a threshold, a courthouse hallway, an HR meeting, a hospital corridor, or a bedroom where truth has finally been spoken, hear me: your beginning is data, not destiny. The labels you were handed are not laws. The rooms that mis-sized you do not get the last word.

Choose sacred order over chronic urgency. Guard your attention like an asset. Reduce the noise and recalibrate to True North. Let your voice heal, on the mic, at the table, in your home. And when you cross your bridge, bring someone with you. That is how you know you're truly free.

I was eight when my mother told me the truth and still chose me. God chose me, too. The girl who cried in that bedroom grew up, got educated, left abuse, rose in tech, calibrated instruments to True North, protected systems and people, advocated for food safety and dignity, married a great man, became Yeye, and built spaces where others could heal with structure, safety, and love.

That isn't just survival. That is Relentless.

About Amirah

Amirah Ansaar is a visionary leader, sacred systems builder, and transformational strategist at the intersection of wellness, technology, and spiritual leadership. As founder of Wellness Revolutionary, she pioneers a "Wellness + Tech Integration" paradigm, helping leaders, families, and faith communities restore sacred order in a digitally driven world.

With more than twenty years in information technology, Amirah merges experience as a Microsoft Cloud Solutions Architect with her training as a National Board-Certified Health & Wellness Coach (NBHWC), an Institute for Integrative Nutrition graduate, and Positive Intelligence® coach. Earlier in her career, she worked in aerospace engineering, from assembly and bench testing to true north calibration of aircraft compasses, and later advanced into cybersecurity, translating complex threat models into human-centered protection.

She is the creator of the Personal Technical WellnessTM Series (Audit → Align → Automate), author of the forthcoming ***Focused: Mastering Attention in a Distracted World***, and a co-author of ***Relentless*** with Lisa Nichols.

As Chief Steward of Sacred Trust Ministries, an ecclesiastically sovereign, faith-based 508(c)(1)(a) sanctuary and ministry alliance, she advances humanitarian service, digital dignity, and sacred governance, strengthening families, protecting the vulnerable, and equipping communities through prayer, education, and practical care.

A media voice for wellness and consciousness, she co-hosts an R&B and Hip Hop radio show, inspiring balance, faith, and freedom. She is also known for a fashion-forward, regal aesthetic, curating garments with the poise of a queen, treating style as visual ministry: order, dignity, and joy made visible.

Amirah lives her message with her husband, a retired Marine veteran known for faith-centered service, and their blended family. Her beloved daughter and two teenage grandchildren (who call her Yeye) are her knowledge, wisdom, and understanding.

Whether guiding executives through an attention reset, helping teams harden their habits without hardening their hearts, or coaching households, as well as communities, back to sacred order, Amirah is relentless about turning insight into lived practice.

Learn more at:
amirahansaar.com
wellnessrevolutionary.com
sacredtrustministries.org

CHAPTER 6

NO MORE SPOTS: HOW DETERMINATION BECAME THE DIFFERENTIATOR

BY BOLA AREMU

The computer roster showed full. Every interview slot for United Airlines was taken, the bidding period had closed, and the career services coordinator at the University of Illinois had already turned me away. Everyone would have understood if I'd accepted that my dream of working in aviation was done before it even took flight. Instead, I put on my best suit, printed five copies of my resume, grabbed my study materials, and planted myself in that waiting room at 8 a.m. sharp.

I refused to leave.

For nine hours, I sat in that waiting lounge, watching interviewers emerge with their scheduled candidates. Each time, I stood up, introduced myself with a firm handshake, and asked the same question. The interviewers stopped making eye contact after hour three. But at 4:30 p.m., something shifted. An interviewer emerged, looked directly at me, and said seven words that changed my life: "You've been here all day. Come in."

That moment of recognition, when determination finally breaks through the wall of "no," became a cornerstone of my career. Eighteen years in aviation. Leadership roles at Boeing and United Airlines. Thirty-five countries visited across six continents (and counting). But none of it would have happened if

I'd listened to that first (second, third, or fourth) rejection, if I'd accepted that final roster, if I'd believed the system when it told me there was no room for me at the table.

I learned that day what I've proven repeatedly throughout my career: half the battle is staying determined, focused, and hopeful.

Some doors won't magically open. But if you're willing to be relentless, truly relentless, you can create an opening where none existed before.

Growing up as the middle child of Nigerian immigrant parents in Chicago shaped this mindset long before I understood its power. My parents exemplified resilience—imagine starting over in your 30s—grad school, new job, new environment, new culture. They understood the sacrifice and determination required to create opportunities for themselves, me, and my sisters.

While other kids went home to watch cartoons after school, I sat in the living room conjugating sentences. Both adult education teachers believed that education was the key to success and a ladder that would lift their children into opportunities they'd crossed an ocean to provide. My mother would say, "Nothing ventured, nothing gained."

My father, a man of few words but profound impact, would drop gems of wisdom and encouragement, especially when one of my sisters or I was in doubt. He would say, "You never know, try and go see."

They were right, but not in the way I expected. What mattered more was the lesson hidden within those evening study sessions: success requires going the extra mile, persisting when others quit, and seeing opportunities where others see obstacles.

That lesson crystallized the day I took my first flight at age six. The moment our British Airways B747 lifted off from Chicago O'Hare bound for London Heathrow, my world exploded beyond the boundaries of the northside of Chicago. In eight hours, I went from a place of familiarity to a world of different foods, accents, traditions, and architecture. I didn't imagine that sixteen years later I'd be working for one of the largest airlines in the world.

But dreams and reality collided hard on September 11, 2001. I was working at United in international revenue management when the industry collapsed overnight. The situation was scary, and the industry's devastation was saddening. The layoff notice came swiftly. The career I'd waited nine hours in a lobby to begin was seemingly over. I thought about pivoting from my passion and moving to a more *stable* industry. The practical move would have been to conclude that aviation wasn't a viable path anymore.

I did pivot, but not away from my vision. Instead of seeing the layoff as an ending, I treated it as an intermission. While the industry recovered, I would upgrade my skills. I applied to the Masters in Integrated Marketing Communications Program at Northwestern, packed my bags, and did something I had wanted to do for years.

I moved to Italy.

There, I studied international marketing and strategic management in the fashion industry. Every day required navigating language barriers, cultural differences, and systems I didn't fully understand. But confusion is temporary if you're willing to persist through it. I quickly gained a global lens that strengthened both my career and worldview.

After a few months in Italy, I received a call from Northwestern.

The decision.

I was accepted into the Master's in IMC Program. I debated delaying the start of the program to spend more time learning in Italy. I didn't want to abandon what I thought was progress. But growth and change are progress, and it was time to move on to the next chapter of my journey, so I moved to Evanston, Illinois, to begin my graduate degree.

My mindset shifted. The blend of experiences expanded my creativity and sharpened my strategy. I leaned into my *How can we?* mantra and embraced innovative integrated marketing methods. I knew I could apply these concepts to any industry for success.

I graduated when the prolonged economic downturn, the dot-com bubble burst, and the effects of 9/11 were still in recovery mode.

I was excited to use my marketing, strategy, and business development expertise in any industry. Only one problem—jobs weren't abundant, especially those in marketing. Months of searching went by, but hope and tenacity remained.

Finally, I found a role that blended sales, strategy, and business development.

The twist: it was back in aviation, at United Airlines' maintenance, repair, and overhaul division. I applied, and the interview was scheduled, only to be cancelled later.

Simple acceptance felt uncomfortable. Was the door really closed, or was there a window open? I called back and learned another role was open. I interviewed—and three weeks later, I was on my way to Northern California to begin a new chapter in aviation.

During the five years at United MRO, I led the launch of the first-of-its-kind fixed-base operator network, expanding United's line maintenance and technical footprint from twenty-four stations to over ninety-eight stations across the globe. This was coupled with leading the relaunch of what was thought to be a dormant product, resulting in thirty-five times the revenue growth within two years.

My direct people leadership began in earnest, leading a team that helped generate more than $300 million in revenue and becoming a trusted advisor behind senior leadership doors.

Five years later, this truth crystallized when I took on a contract role at one of the biggest financial institutions in the world.

They initially refused to even interview me.

"She doesn't have financial industry experience," they told my recruiter.

But the recruiter was relentless, too, insisting that they at least meet me. I wore my best Brooks Brothers suit to that interview, the same mindset I'd carried into the United Airlines waiting room more than a decade earlier.

Within twenty-four hours, I had an offer.

Within two months, they extended my contract with a 10 percent raise.

Within a year, they offered me a full-time position.

Why? Because I leveraged my IMC principles, my standard process knowledge that I learned in aviation, and my creativity to bring comprehensive strategies to target new business and provide fresh perspectives to stale problems.

A new opportunity arose again in aviation at the Oakland International Airport.

This proved to be my most defining test thus far.

Three months into the job, the airport director approached me with an assignment that made my jaw drop. “We need you to lead the launch of an airline. This will be the first regularly scheduled non-stop international service in our airport’s history. The community has been demanding this for years, including our Board.”

I wanted to say that I wasn’t ready—new employee, tight timelines, huge stakes, a foreign carrier entering a new market. Then I remembered my parents’ words about endeavoring and pursuing the venture.

The challenge demanded resourcefulness: limited budgets, tight timelines, internal and external coordination, and even drawing on old design skills. Yes, the stakes were high, and the impact could be profound.

It took a village. I leveraged relationships with local, regional, and national travel bureaus. I couldn’t hire a big agency, so I helped design collateral. It took cross-functional teaming. It took out-of-the box thinking. It took collaboration. And it even took a bit of lobbying.

Launch day arrived. When that first Norwegian Airlines flight lifted off from Oakland to Stockholm, carrying a load of passengers on a new B787 Dreamliner, I felt the magnitude of what we had built—a campaign that generated headlines across continents and became one of the most complex and rewarding projects of my career. It proved that relentlessness isn’t only about working harder or being smarter—it’s about refusing to accept “impossible.” It was one of the most incredible feelings of accomplishment and gratitude.

A new opportunity arose. I took it.

Then, after a two-year stint at the largest California utility company, I felt a pull back into aviation. Shortly afterwards, I moved to Texas with an offer from Boeing to join their product line management team for aviation oils and lubricants.

In this role, I managed the supplier relationships of major organizations such as Shell, BP, and ExxonMobil. I loved the dynamic nature of the role because I could apply my entrepreneurial mindset to grow the business. I oversaw sales, P&L, and marketing for my product lines. It was like running a mini business within a larger business.

Initially, it wasn't easy. Some relationships were broken and seemingly irreparable, revenue was down, and engagement was low. It would take much more than a few mediation meetings to solve. I took a step back and started with the ultimate goal. From there, I built a strategy that included gathering information, understanding the expectations of external partners, the goals of key internal stakeholders, and the needs of the ultimate customer. From this, I could hone in on the gaps and begin to craft a viable solution. The positive results were evident within a year. Regular cadences of business reviews, the creation of incentive structures, increased face-to-face visits, status checks, collaboration meetings, shared goals, accountability, and mutual wins were implemented from the overarching strategy.

This strategy, along with the *How can we?* spirit resulted in millions of dollars in revenue growth, improved supplier-distributor relationships that directly impacted the bottom line, and my receipt of a special award of business growth recognition from Exxon.

Reaching the top of a mountain requires multiple steps. It's the same with big goals. Even when the task seems insurmountable, create a plan and take it piece by piece.

This role exposed me to other opportunities, and I continued my growth journey. I applied to one of Boeing's top leadership development programs, where only 2 percent were selected. With my dad as my champion, I applied.

I was selected.

The program transformed my understanding of leadership. I learned that being relentless has many facets. It means building networks of support that amplify your efforts. It means recognizing that success is not a singular function. It requires champions, mentors, allies, and sometimes even constructive critics who push you to be better. Every breakthrough I've experienced has come not from solo effort, but from creating conditions where collective success is possible.

More doors have opened since, including leading a go-to-market launch of a Boeing-patented product, building customer support programs for commercial airline customers, and leading a team that supports parts and system solutions for global distribution.

Today, I lead a marketing consulting firm. I am the founder of Powerhouse Consulting, where I partner with corporate leaders to drive multimillion-dollar sales growth through marketing, sales alignment, and product development.

I continue to bring an entrepreneurial mindset when approaching business problems, and I refuse to accept artificial limitations.

When clients doubt whether their *impossible* goals are achievable, I help them reframe the path forward and show them the strategy that makes it possible.

The thread connecting every breakthrough, every shattered barrier, every impossible-to-possible transformation is this: I became relentless about refusing to quit when quitting would have been easy. Not stubborn—stubborn people keep doing the same thing, expecting different results. Relentless people find new routes to the same destination. When the front door closes, we check the windows. When the windows are locked, we build our own door.

But here's what no success story tells you: being relentless can be exhausting. There were nights in Italy when I questioned why I was in a foreign country instead of building a "safe" career back home. There were moments in corporate when I wondered if the pieces would come together after so much effort. Many days, I relied upon my closest champions, my network of mentors, for support, encouragement, and advice.

The difference between those who break through and those who break down isn't that we don't feel the weight; it's that we've learned to carry it differently. We celebrate small wins because we know progress is success. We build support networks because we know isolation is the enemy of persistence. We share our stories because we know someone else is sitting beside themself, wondering if they should quit, and they need to hear that the struggle is universal, the journey is non-linear, but the breakthrough is possible.

If you're standing at the edge of your own impossible moment, if you're being told you are not a fit, don't have the connections, or it's not the right time, know this: those are opinions, not facts. Often, the gap between where you are and where you want to be is simply tenacity. Every person who's ever told you "No" was just announcing that they'd reached the limit of their imagination, not yours.

You don't need the perfect circumstances to begin. Not all of the answers need to be checked before you begin building. The ambiguity is part of the journey, and moving forward provides clarity. Growth can be quite uncomfortable, but the reward is undeniable.

But if you're willing to sit in that waiting room when everyone else has gone home, if you're ready to ask, "How can I?" instead of accepting "You can't," if you can see rejection as redirection and obstacles as opportunities, then you already have the foundation. The only question that matters is this: How relentless are you willing to be?

The answer to that question will determine whether your impossible remains impossible or becomes your inevitability. I chose inevitability. I'm still choosing it every day. And you can too. Your breakthrough is not a matter of if. It's a matter of when you decide that quitting is the only impossible thing.

Your next decision can change everything. Be relentless.

About Oyebola (Bola)

Bola Aremu is the founder and CEO of Powerhouse Consulting, where she partners with corporate leaders to help them achieve multi-million-dollar growth through marketing, sales alignment, and product development. A strategist at the intersection of insight, execution, and leadership, Bola's specialties include product launches, partnership management, and P/L supervision.

With more than two decades of experience driving revenue transformation, Bola is known for her ability to bring clarity to complex organizational challenges. Her career spans aviation, energy, consumer packaged goods, financial services, and business services—industries where she has repeatedly delivered results in high-stakes, highly regulated, and highly competitive environments.

In her corporate career, Bola has served in strategic leadership roles at The Boeing Company, where she has managed multimillion-dollar product portfolios, led global go-to-market strategies for aviation lubricants, overseen complex supplier partnerships with ExxonMobil, Shell, and BP, and led an international team supporting customized solutions for commercial, government, and business aviation customers.

Prior to Boeing, Bola held key roles at Pacific Gas & Electric, where she led integrated marketing strategy for more than 350,000 customers and developed a comprehensive GTM plan for the West Coast Energy Center in San Francisco. At the Port of Oakland, she drove the launch of the airport's first regularly scheduled nonstop B787 service to Europe, generating over $100M in travel impact within the first year while improving customer wait time experience by 33 percent.

Her earlier work at BlackRock and United Airlines solidified her expertise in product marketing, revenue management, sales support, and event strategy—culminating in strategic wins such as exceeding $300M revenue goals and launching high-margin aviation products.

Bola holds a Master's in Integrated Marketing from Northwestern University, a Bachelor's in Business Administration from the University of Illinois, certificates in Corporate Finance and Social Media Marketing Strategy from UC Berkeley and

Cornell, respectively, and completed coursework in international marketing & strategic management in fashion from Bocconi University in Italy. She is fluent in the language of business building—and conversational in Italian and Spanish.

Born and raised in Chicago, she was instilled with education, resilience, and faith. In her spare time, Bola enjoys hiking, HIIT training, investing, and football. Having traveled to over 35 countries, she is a global travel connoisseur and believes that "travel is her addiction and her therapy."

"Life is too short for mediocrity. Whatever you do, make it great!" – Bola Aremu

Connect at: linkedin.com/in/bolaaremu

CHAPTER 7

PREPARED TO SPEAK: A GENTLE REVOLUTION

BY JANI DECENA-WHITE

WASHINGTON HEIGHTS, 1980

Washington Heights doesn't sleep. Little Dominican Republic, they call it. It hums a beautiful, vibrant, layered Afro-Caribbean rhythm.

Voices travel across fire escapes. Radios compete. People watch each other live, lifting one another up, falling out, dreaming in proximity. Every window exhales a life.

My sister and I pressed our faces to the window. The sidewalk was theater. The block was energy. Salsa and merengue floated up from the street through open windows, bled through thin apartment walls, climbed stairwells that carried sound like memory.

Music was always there.

But the sweetest music came when my mother was happy.

On those days, she sang boleros. Slow, soulful songs about lost love and a far-away home. She had always dreamed of being a singer. When she sang, our bodies knew before our minds did. Something softened. Something reset. If we woke to her gorgeous, mournful voice, we knew it would be a good day.

Peace, when it came, was musical.

* * *

My mother was a strong, proud Puerto Rican woman carrying childhood trauma, abandonment, two divorces carved into her heart, and the weight of raising three daughters alone in a community that could eat us alive.

In her experience, the world could not be trusted. We had to be educated. Independent. Prepared.

I can still hear her: "A man is not a plan."

But we learned a paradox early.

She wanted us strong, yet we were not allowed our own thoughts. If we spoke at the wrong time, thought differently, questioned what she believed was right, the storm arrived quickly.

As the oldest, I caught it most often.

Because I wasn't silent.

I questioned. I talked back, trying to reason with a woman fighting her demons. And it cost me blows that left marks on my body, though none as deep as her words.

* * *

One hot and humid June, 1980. End of the school year. The kind of afternoon where laughter comes easily because you forget to be careful.

I was fifteen. I had invited a friend over after school. We were in the living room, my sisters nearby, laughing. Real laughter, the kind that makes you feel, for a moment, like a normal girl with a normal life.

Then I heard her footsteps.

My mother's frame filled the doorway. Her eyes went to my friend first, then to me. And her face shifted into something I recognized, something that made my stomach drop before she said a word.

"*Pero tú sí eres basura.*"

Slow. Drawn out. Disgusted.

But. You. Really. Are. Garbage.

I watched my friend's face change. Watched her grab her things. Watched her rush down the long hallway and out of my apartment like it was on fire.

And something in me, the part that had been beaten down a hundred times but hadn't learned to stay down, stepped forward.

"Mami… I am not garbage."

The belt was already in the air.

* * *

Years later, I would understand: fighting back was not the most relentless thing I ever did. It was refusing to let harshness win by becoming it.

Gentleness would become my fiercer revolution.

* * *

THE BODY REMEMBERS

That afternoon wasn't the first time she called me that word. It was just the first time she said it with a witness.

In private, these names were the wallpaper of my childhood:

Inoportuna: speaks at the wrong time.

Basura: should be thrown away.

Inútil: useless, worthless.

The muffled sound of Héctor Lavoe played somewhere in the building. The smell of someone's mother's cooking drifted through the window. The sounds of joy and life, outside.

While inside, I was reminded my voice was dangerous. That my presence was a problem. That disappearing was safer than wanting.

Maybe you know that girl. Maybe you were her.

Maybe you are still her, in a grown woman's body, flinching at the memory of someone who taught you that taking up space came with a cost.

THE COST OF QUIET

Learning to be quiet taught me how to navigate danger. But it did not teach me how to name it.

There were things I stayed silent about. Touches that lingered too long. Closeness that crossed lines. Pulls onto laps. Moments that made my body tense before my mind could catch up. I didn't have language for that.

When I told, I was called an *exagerada*, or a liar.

So, I stopped telling.

So many of us grow up skilled at accommodation but without language for ourselves. We are taught to be agreeable, to manage other people's comfort, to endure what feels wrong without naming it, because naming it once brought punishment, dismissal, or shame. We received instructions to be quiet, to keep family business out of the street, to protect people who were *good*.

Without words for self-advocacy, we smile, redirect, absorb, shrink, and are silenced.

When a woman has learned that speaking carries risk, encouragement alone will never be enough. Before she can speak freely, she has to learn how to trust herself again.

What I know is silence is not self-care. It's self-erasure disguised as peace.

RELENTLESSNESS AS KINDNESS

I never experienced my questions as disobedience or as being difficult. I was trying to understand my mother, her pain, her volatility. I was trying to protect myself and my sisters from being worn down by words that cut deeper than hands.

I knew she was hurting and afraid. I knew her intentions were rooted in love.

I also knew that fear and guilt were not teaching us how to be whole.

We needed someone to speak to who we could become, not to who we were in our supposed worst moments.

I didn't want to become what had shaped me, so I chose to become careful with power, to build rooms where questions don't carry consequence, to teach without humiliation or injury.

My revolt would be kindness.

* * *

I saw what this meant in my classroom before I gave it language.

One student, brilliant, capable, terrified, started every answer with "I'm sorry, but..." or "This might be wrong, but..." Her voice got smaller with each sentence, as if apologizing for taking up air.

I waited. I let her finish without the raised eyebrow or the impatient sigh she seemed to be bracing for. Then I said, simply: "You don't have to apologize for being right."

She looked at me like no one had ever given her that space.

For the rest of the semester, she raised her hand. No apology. No disclaimer. Just her voice, clear and sure.

Gentleness creates the conditions where courage becomes possible.

WHAT SHE PLANTED

At home, even when I could leave, I stayed, forever trying to prove a worth that was never acknowledged until my mother's last year. Her voice, my inner critic.

My mother believed harshness was the only way to ensure we would listen. Perhaps her vigilance was her way of proving her own worth. If we were above reproach, so was she.

But I have learned that gentleness reaches deeper than fear ever could.

We rise to the belief of those who reflect us.

Thankfully, wherever we moved, we found a church. It allowed the Word to reach me, to know deep inside that God was near.

"For I know the plans I have for you," declares the Lord. "Plans to prosper you and not to harm you. Plans to give you hope and a future."

I thank Mami for that, though it would take years, my sister, Mildred's prayers, and a few women who shared God's grace before I understood. I was worthy of more.

God gave me the relentless audacity of hope.

THE YES THAT CHANGED EVERYTHING

There is an old truth: harshness speaks to the fool. It assumes force is the only way to be heard. Gentleness speaks to the queen. It trusts she is capable of rising.

I had to learn to speak to the queen in myself before I could speak to her in anyone else.

Now, the old voices no longer lead. They remain behind me, remnants of who I was, not evidence of who I am.

Yet when the opportunity came, I hesitated. I said, "That's a wild dream. Maybe one day."

Lisa Nichols had created *When My Soul Speaks* on Broadway. The deadline to become a producer had passed. That old voice said: Girl. You are too late. You missed it. Not for you.

But there was another voice. Quieter. The queen, who had survived every room that tried to shrink her, said, "Try."

So I reached out to Lisa's best friend. She gave me contact information for Lisa's assistant. I called. I emailed. I added my picture.

I opened my heart and my mouth.

I reached out the way gentleness had taught me: with clarity and trust that the right door would recognize me.

My phone rang. It was Lisa Nichols. Not her team or assistant. Lisa.

She told me she'd said to her team, "Let me speak with her. She's from my campus. She's here because of her relationship with me."

Her first words to me were, "Congratulations on being radical. On being bold."

My voice put me in New York at a private producer's event. On the red carpet. Standing on stage with thirty producers, eighty percent of them Black women, in what was said might be one of the highest Black women producer events ever created on Broadway.

On one call, Lisa shared, "Nothing that ever gave me a huge return felt safe on the front end."

She was right.

The woman who learned to speak gently to herself became the woman who could speak boldly to anyone.

THE ROOMS I BUILT

Over the years, I have come to know my worth and my power. However, I didn't start healed. I didn't start fearless and confident. I just started anyway.

At twenty-two, I walked through CUNY City College's neo-Gothic arches, not to my graduate classes or advisor's office, but to my own classroom.

I took a deep breath before I walked in.

The students looked tired, distracted. I felt them straighten as I moved toward the front desk, set my things down, turned to the board, and wrote my name, still unsure about facing them.

When I turned around, I saw it. The smile. The wonder. The curiosity. Faces that looked like mine. Expressions asking without words: Is this the professor?

I didn't know it then, but I would hear it for decades: "I love that you're Latina."

"I've never had a professor who looked like me."

"You make me believe in myself."

"Thank you for listening."

My presence spoke. It gave permission.

That was decades ago. I was carrying every wound. I just refused to let the wounds lead.

Since then, I have built businesses, a real estate portfolio, spoken on stages across continents. I raised three children who speak their minds without flinching. I have been married thirty-four years to a man who still cherishes me.

Here is what I know. The woman who waits until she feels ready will wait forever. The woman who moves before she feels ready builds a life other women will still be dreaming about.

The women who transform are not just the ones who started long ago. They are the ones who decide, sometimes in a single afternoon, that their next chapter will not be written by the names or rooms that tried to shrink them.

I am transforming what my mother started. I am building without breaking. And every woman I serve becomes proof that the cycle can end, gently, fiercely, permanently, in a single generation.

THE INVITATION

I have held space for over seven thousand women learning to trust their own voices.

Women at the beginning of their journeys. Women who looked successful yet felt constrained. Women whose competence was shaped by pressure, not permission.

They came speaking as though they were apologizing. They couldn't see what silence was costing them. In dollars. In impact. In peace of mind. In years.

They came carrying what they had never been able to put down: money they couldn't ask for, opportunities they didn't pursue, ideas stolen by colleagues who spoke first, decades of swallowed words sitting in their bodies like stones.

A woman messaged me after one session: "I caught myself apologizing in a conversation, for nothing. And I heard your voice: *What are you apologizing for?* I stopped mid-sentence. That's the first time in my life I've done that."

One shift. Decades of patterns, interrupted. Two months later, she negotiated a raise she'd been afraid to ask for. And got it.

Another wrote: "I had something to say, but fear made it feel impossible. With Jani's guidance, I found courage. I applied for my dream job and negotiated based on what we determined my work was worth. Result: the leadership role I deserved and $30,000 over initial offer."

Another launched the business she'd been planning for two years.

Another said, "You may be saving my marriage. He genuinely didn't get it."

What surprises them is how it begins. They expect fierce pressure and aggression. They find gentleness instead.

And once the walls come down, we do the real work: positioning, negotiation, visibility, executive presence. Then they can claim the rooms they've been circling, the stages they've been watching others claim, the compensation that matches their contribution.

They come to me stuck. They leave prepared for the life they'd convinced themselves wasn't for women like them. For the business. The platform. The relationship. The raise. The promotion.

There's something that happens in just the first thirty days. A shift my clients describe as putting down a weight they didn't know they were carrying. And, not one woman who has done the work has ever wished she'd waited longer to begin.

My work is helping women remember what my mentor once said: *God is not trying to play you with your dreams.* So, I walk beside them into the rooms, onto the stages, and through the doors where they're ready to be seen.

If you are a woman who still edits herself before she speaks, who prepares endlessly but hesitates at the moment of visibility, who knows her voice matters but cannot seem to trust it in the rooms that matter most, something in these pages was written for you.

That is not a coincidence. It's recognition of unwanted patterns.

* * *

You are someone's answered prayer.

Your voice carries what someone needs to hear. Every day you stay silent, you're burying your talents in the ground.

That is not why you have them.

Silence is not self-care. It's self-erasure disguised as peace.

Your silence costs more than you know, and you're not the only one paying. But courage can be learned.

There is a queen in you who has survived every room that tried to shrink her. She's asking: *Why not now?*

It's time to stop being a best-kept secret.

Be relentless.

Your bold and courageous era is waiting.

About Jani

Founder and CEO, Prepared to Speak™ and Empowered Impact Experience | Communication & Visibility Strategist | Keynote Speaker

Jani Decena-White believes silence is the most expensive thing a woman will ever pay for, and she's rarely the only one paying.

Her daughter is watching. The women around her are watching. Every time a woman swallows her words, she teaches someone else to swallow theirs. The silence becomes inheritance. The shrinking becomes legacy. Jani has spent thirty years in a revolution to break that cycle for every woman and girl who comes after.

Through Prepared to Speak™, she has guided thousands of women to use their voices as strategic tools, in negotiations, on stages, and in the conversations that shape their lives.

But this work goes deeper than strategy. Many women come to Jani holding dreams they've never given themselves permission to pursue, held back by a lack of trust in themselves, fractured relationships, or years of believing they weren't worthy of more. Jani helps them remember the truth: they are of immeasurable worth to God, and that worth doesn't need to be earned. It needs to be claimed.

Her approach is different. Where others teach performance, Jani teaches presence rooted in purpose, not perfection. Where others offer frameworks and send you on your way, Jani stays. She calls it a gentle revolution, one that does more than change a woman's life—it redirects her entire lineage.

Her career proves what becomes possible when a woman refuses to stay silent. For thirty years, she taught, mentored, and led in classrooms, boardrooms, coaching rooms, and on stages. She built programs that changed lives, a seven-figure real estate portfolio, and multiple businesses, and in 2024, became a Broadway co-producer.

Her signature offering is Empowered Impact, an exclusive one-to-one coaching partnership with Jani in your corner, weekly, helping you close the gap between where you are and where you know you belong. Women who want inspiration have options. Women who want execution and results choose this.

Jani is a proud Latina: Boricua and Dominicana. Her faith anchors everything. She believes what scripture says: God did not give us a spirit of fear, but of power, love, and a sound mind.

She has made it her life's work to help women live like they believe it too.

janiwhite.co
Your bold and courageous era is waiting.

CHAPTER 8

WHEN THE GROUND GIVES WAY: HOW LOSING EVERYTHING BECAME MY FOUNDATION

BY SHERYL ROY DUNBAR-DIXON

The knock on my door came at 7:15 a.m. In that suspended moment between sleep and consciousness, I knew. Before my hand reached the door, peering through the curtains, before seeing the two policemen, before my world tilted off its axis, I knew.

I had spent the entire night tossing and turning as my husband did not come home. No one had seen him or knew of his whereabouts, and now the police were outside.

They had found his body. On him was my photo and a blank cheque I had given him to pay for his medical. My heart stopped, my world stopped.

Suddenly, I replayed our last conversation the previous day. He had called me whilst I was at work. I thought it was just one of his usual phone calls. He ended the call with the words 'keep on keeping on.' It hit me like a ton of bricks that with those words, he had said goodbye.

Keep on keeping on. Those four words would become my North Star through decades of reinvention, through countries and careers, through discrimination and divorce. But in that moment, sitting on the edge of my bed in Jamaica with my sleeping child in the next room, those words felt like a cruel joke. How does a young widow with a baby keep on keeping on when the ground beneath her feet has turned to quicksand?

Our strict religious upbringing, what I now recognize as a doomsday cult, had rules about everything from who you could love, how you could love them, and what dreams were acceptable to have. When the elders discovered our relationship, they didn't just disapprove; they actively separated us, triggering the mental health crisis that landed him in that sterile facility with its locked doors and medicated silence. With this desperately sad turn of events, at the request of his family, I was allowed to visit him at the mental institution. I was deemed the only hope to fix this situation, which I hadn't caused.

Our first dates consisted of walks around the hospital grounds, conversations interrupted by medication schedules, hope blooming despite the institutional walls surrounding us. When he recovered, we married soon after. Our union was accepted, but the damage was done. The confident young man I'd fallen for struggled to hold jobs. The weight of the religious obligations, combined with his ongoing mental health challenges, pressed down on him daily. I became the primary earner, juggling work in commercial banking with caring for our new baby and supporting a husband whose light grew dimmer each day.

That final phone call came after years of him trying to be what everyone expected as a provider, spiritual head, and man who fit the mold our religion demanded. "I can't do it anymore," he'd say, and I'd reassure him we'd figure it out together. We always did. Except this time, we wouldn't.

THE PRISON OF PARADISE

Growing up in our religious community was like living in a beautiful cage. Jamaica's lush landscapes surrounded us, but our world was small, controlled, and suffocating. The leaders preached that the end of the world was imminent. Why pursue education when Armageddon was around the corner? Why build a career when material success was evidence of spiritual weakness? Why dream when dreams were just distractions from preparing for paradise?

By age thirty-five, I realized a terrifying truth: I had no personal dreams. None. Every aspiration had been handed to me by the organization, every goal filtered through their lens of acceptable ambition. It would take me ten years to deprogram, to excavate my own desires from beneath layers of conditioning. But that realization came later. First, I had to survive.

A year after burying my first husband, I remarried. The community was supportive—a widow needed protection, after all. Within months, we decided to move to the United Kingdom, where my husband was born, hoping it would give us a fresh start. Armed with just a one-way ticket and his certainty that God would provide, I packed our lives into suitcases, lifted my toddler onto my hip, and boarded a plane to London with winter approaching and no idea what awaited us.

WHEN CREDENTIALS DON'T CROSS BORDERS

London in November hit like a physical assault. The cold penetrated every layer of tropical clothing I'd packed. The gray sky pressed down like a lid on a pot, trapping us in a monochrome world so different from Jamaica's technicolor vibrancy. But the weather was the least of my challenges.

My commercial banking experience? Worthless. My education? Not recognized. My professional network? An ocean away. For two years, two soul-crushing, dignity-stripping years, I couldn't find professional work. Every interview ended the same way. They'd look at my brown skin, hear my accent, see *Jamaica* on my resume, and suddenly the position would be "already filled," or I'd be "overqualified," or they'd need someone with "local experience."

Two years of rejection letters. Two years of watching our savings evaporate. Two years of my husband's frustration grew as his own job search proved equally fruitless. Two years of wondering if I'd made the biggest mistake of my life following him to this cold, unwelcoming country.

Finally, I surrendered my pride. I signed up with an employment agency for temp work. They were surprised by my credentials, but I made it clear I was willing to consider anything. Following further rejections of my CV by potential employers, the agency came across a position I was sure I would be accepted for: a kitchen hand. Washing dishes.

The interviewer, barely able to hide his surprise at my credentials, hired me on the spot. "Are you sure you want this?" he asked. I wanted to scream that no, I didn't want to stand for eight hours scrubbing pots, that I'd managed high net worth clients, that I was worth more than minimum wage and waterlogged hands. Instead, I said, "I need local references."

That kitchen job became my foothold. Three months of showing up early, staying late, proving my reliability. Armed with that single local reference, I applied for a foreign exchange position at Heathrow Airport. Numbers were numbers, whether in Jamaican or British currency. They hired me, and suddenly I could breathe again. Not deeply, not freely, but enough to keep moving forward.

THE LONG CLIMB FROM THE BOTTOM

The airport job ended when childcare became impossible. The shifts were erratic, and I found myself again at the bottom, this time as a filing clerk for the local council. Filing. Alphabetizing. Fetching coffee. Watching less qualified colleagues advance while I remained invisible, just another immigrant grateful for any job.

But I'd learned something in that restaurant kitchen: pride was a luxury I couldn't afford, but tenacity was free. Every evening, I attended night college. Retraining. Adapting. Proving myself over and over in ways my colleagues never had to. I was playing their game now, by their rules, but with twice the determination.

The filing clerk became an administrative assistant. The assistant became an officer. The officer became a team leader. Each promotion felt like climbing Everest in flip-flops; possible, but unnecessarily difficult. Finally, I achieved the role of Principal Officer, representing the council in court for taxation cases. From washing dishes to arguing legal precedents, the journey had taken eleven years.

Then they made me redundant. Blindsided.

"Restructuring," they called it. "Nothing personal." But when you're one of the few Black faces in leadership, when you've consistently outperformed your targets, when your reviews are exemplary, and you're still the one chosen for redundancy. It's personal. It was a slap in the face that should have knocked me down. Instead, it woke me up.

THE BUSINESS OF SURVIVAL

The redundancy shook me enough. Enough to finally act on the business degree I'd earned at night school. Enough to bet on myself instead of waiting for an organization to value me. Enough to ensure no one could ever pull the rug out from under me again.

I succeeded in finding alternative employment. Following long days in a new role, I worked tirelessly during the evenings to set up the business. Starting a business in the UK felt like signing up for another fight. But I'd been fighting uphill for so long, the gradient barely registered anymore.

The business grew slowly, then suddenly. The tenacity that had carried me from that knock on the door through continents and careers became my competitive advantage. Where others saw obstacles, I saw normal Tuesday problems. Where others might quit, I simply didn't know how.

The company I'd started from my kitchen table now employed others. The woman who'd once washed dishes to get a reference now mentored. The immigrant who'd been told her credentials were worthless now had clients. The redundancy that might have diminished me had instead revealed what I was truly capable of.

BREAKING CYCLES, BUILDING FUTURES

Perhaps the greatest test of my tenacity came not in boardrooms or courtrooms, but in my son's classroom. The British education system, which I'd discovered was far behind Jamaica's at the primary level, was failing him. I sent him to school but quietly taught him at home. He was ahead of his peers and outperformed them in exams, but this was not recognised at the secondary school level. Teachers saw a Black boy from a single-parent home and adjusted their expectations accordingly. When he acted out from boredom, they labeled him problematic rather than gifted.

I refused to let their limited vision become his reality. I challenged assessments, demanded testing, and advocated relentlessly until they recognized what I'd always known. My son was gifted and talented, simply unchallenged. The system that had tried to pipeline him toward low expectations instead had to create advanced programming to match his abilities.

Today, he's a sought-after professional at a prestigious media company, headhunted for his expertise. When colleagues express surprise at his achievements, he smiles and says he had no choice but to excel. His mother wouldn't accept anything less. He's right. I'd fought too hard for him to inherit anything but excellence as his birthright.

THE COURAGE TO CHOOSE YOURSELF

My second marriage ended not with a tragic phone call but with a quiet recognition that staying was killing me slowly. The religious community that had shaped and constrained my early life didn't accept divorce. When I filed the papers, friends scattered like startled birds. The phone stopped ringing. The invitations ceased. In a foreign country, with no family or community, I faced an isolation that felt complete.

But here's what I learned in that silence: sometimes losing everything is the only way to find out what's truly yours. The faith that remained when the institution fell away. The strength that endured when the support system vanished. The dreams that finally had space to grow when no one else's expectations crowded them out.

I think about that young woman receiving that devastating knock on the door, cradling her baby while her world collapsed. I want to tell her that "keep on keeping on" would become more than last words. They'd become a philosophy that would carry her across oceans, through discrimination, past redundancy, beyond divorce, into a life she couldn't have imagined.

I want to tell her that tenacity isn't about being strong all the time. It's about being willing to wash dishes when you've managed millions. It's about studying by lamplight when your eyes burn with exhaustion. It's about advocating for your child when the whole system is stacked against him. It's about leaving a marriage when staying means spiritual death. It's about building something from nothing, over and over, until "nothing" no longer scares you.

THE IMPRINT WE LEAVE

When I joined this project, Lisa Nichols asked why I wanted to share my story. I told her I wanted to leave an imprint. Not because my pain was unique—pain never is. Not because my triumph was extraordinary. Triumph is always possible. But because someone needs to know that when you're standing in the rubble of your life, when everyone has written you off, when the ground gives way beneath your feet, you're capable of much more than you know.

Follow your heart, even when it leads you away from everything familiar. Be true to who you are, even when who you are doesn't fit anyone else's mold. And when life tells you to quit, when circumstances scream that you've lost, when everyone, including yourself, doubts you can continue—keep on keeping on.

Those four words, spoken by a desperate man in his darkest hour, became the foundation of a life built on tenacity. They carried a young widow from Jamaica to London, from kitchen sink to courtroom, from redundancy to entrepreneurship, from isolation to impact. They're my gift to you now, wrapped in my story but meant for your journey.

Your circumstances don't define you. Your next decision does. And if you're reading this while standing in your own rubble, wondering how to take the next step, remember: you don't have to see the whole staircase. You just have to keep on keeping on.

The ground will solidify beneath your feet. Not because life gets easier, but because you get stronger. Not because obstacles disappear, but because you become relentless in moving through them. Not because anyone gives you permission to succeed, but because you finally stop asking for it.

This is what tenacity looks like: not a superhuman strength, but a very human refusal to quit. Not an absence of fear, but action in its presence. Not a guarantee of success, but a guarantee that failure won't have the last word.

You're capable of much more than you know. I'm living proof. And tomorrow, if you choose to keep on keeping on, you will be too.

About Sheryl

Sheryl is a confident professional with a strong track record of success, having worked in a variety of roles at strategic and operational levels within the private and public sectors. Her diverse career history spans over 30 years, ranging from commercial banking to economic development and regeneration. Within Local Authority, Sheryl served as Principal Revenues Officer, where she thrived as a strong leader, managed difficult debt recovery processes, and successfully led her team to achieve stringent collection targets each year.

Later, working at a strategic level within Economic Development, Sheryl was selected to lead various high-profile government-funded programmes. She particularly enjoyed her role in supporting businesses to win more contracts, refine their business plans, and encourage entrepreneurship. This role showcased her natural ability to develop effective partnership approaches, whilst working with external partner organisations, toward shared objectives.

For over 10 years, Sheryl juggled full-time employment with a growing side business in Construction and Property Services. During the past year, she has opted for a full return to the private sector. As co-founder and Managing Director of a successful company, Sheryl is responsible for organisational strategy, finance, and implementing systems and technology.

Alongside this, Sheryl is a successful property investor and works collaboratively to support other investors in building their own property portfolios.

Sheryl has a success mindset and advocates personal growth and empowerment. She is a passionate speaker and mentor who connects easily with others. Her impressive achievements are a testament to her unwavering commitment to excellence, whilst embracing challenges with dignity, focus, and resilience.

Outside of work, Sheryl enjoys various pastimes, including travel, nature, and high-performance sports cars.

Connect with Sheryl at: linkedin.com/in/sheryl-dixon

CHAPTER 9

BUILDING BRIDGES THROUGH THE STORM

BY DENEEN WHITE

The hurricane rain hammered against the windows of my Pennsylvania home that August morning, a fitting soundtrack for what I was about to share. Nature has a way of mirroring the lessons we need most. The pounding rain and whipping winds reminded me that leadership, like weather, demands both preparation and the ability to adapt when storms come uninvited. Some of the greatest truths arrive disguised in thunder, testing our ability to endure while pushing us toward growth.

For years, I have helped entrepreneurs and entertainment professionals confront what I call the precipice of fear. Most people assume their struggle lies in a lack of ambition or drive. They believe they just need more motivation. But that's not the real barrier. The obstacle isn't the height of their dreams. It's the depth of their self-doubt, carved by past mistakes and disappointments. These doubts erode belief in themselves, leaving them frozen at the edge of possibility. They want to leap, yet they can't take the first step.

My calling is to build bridges that help them cross.

THE COST OF NOT PAUSING

Every day in business, I make a choice many people consider inefficient: I pause. Not the hesitation of fear or uncertainty, but a deliberate pause to actually see the person in front of me. That one practice has reshaped my career and touched the lives of more than 10,000 people in the entertainment industry. Pausing taught me that empathy isn't a soft skill. It's a superpower.

Not long ago, I sat across from a client who puzzled my entire team. The project details were solid, the terms were fair, and the opportunity clear. Yet they kept delaying, finding new reasons not to move forward. Most professionals would have pressed harder—sell more, push more, close faster. Instead, I stopped.

"This isn't really about the contract, is it?" I asked gently.

Their shoulders dropped. For the first time in weeks of discussions, they met my eyes. "The last time I trusted someone with a project like this, I lost everything."

That one pause changed everything. We spent the next hour not reviewing terms, but unpacking fears. I validated their concerns. I shared my own painful experiences with betrayal in business. Most importantly, I showed them their past didn't have to dictate their future.

The deal eventually closed, but more than that, a real relationship was born. That client went on to refer three others, each one saying nearly the same words: "You need to work with Deneen. She actually cares."

That is the power of the pause. While others rush to close deals, I choose to invest in understanding the human being across from me. It isn't always the fastest path, but it is always the most sustainable one. Because when people feel genuinely seen and heard, they don't just sign contracts. They become advocates, partners, even lifelong friends.

THREE DEATHS AND A REBIRTH

I didn't develop empathy in boardrooms or at leadership seminars. I built it in hospital rooms—most profoundly during my mother's battle with stage four breast cancer. Of all the defining moments in my life, three stand out, but none taught me more than watching her confront death with courage.

During those long days and sleepless nights, I learned that listening, truly listening, not just hearing words, could be as healing as medicine. My mother shared stories, regrets, dreams, and fears she had never voiced before. In her vulnerability, I discovered a truth that would reshape how I lead: everyone is fighting a battle invisible to the world.

One night, she held my hand tightly and whispered, "I'm not afraid of dying. I'm afraid of not being remembered for who I really was." That confession broke me open. I realized how often people move through life unseen, unheard, unknown. We present polished professional facades while our real selves and struggles remain hidden in the shadows.

After she passed, I carried that lesson into every interaction. When team members wrestled with comparison or self-doubt, I remembered her fear of being forgotten. When clients resisted change, I recalled her worry about leaving things unfinished. When colleagues seemed abrasive, I asked myself what pain they might be carrying beneath the surface.

That perspective didn't just make me a better leader. It made me a bridge builder. Because once you realize everyone shoulders invisible burdens, you stop trying to push them across the bridge. Instead, you stand with them until they find the strength to cross on their own.

THE DENTAL OFFICE LESSON

Sometimes our greatest strengths double as our greatest limitations. I discovered this early in my career at a dental office. My role at the front desk went far beyond checking in patients. Anxious patients found comfort in my words. Elderly clients felt genuinely heard. Children who usually dreaded the dentist actually looked forward to visits. The dentist himself told me I had transformed the atmosphere of his practice. Treatment acceptance rates soared, and business thrived.

So when the office manager position opened, I assumed the promotion was mine. After all, I had been performing many of the duties already—staying late, reorganizing schedules, suggesting systems that improved efficiency by thirty percent. The interview felt like a formality.

Then came the meeting that reshaped my view of mentorship. The dentist called me into his office.

"Deneen, you're too valuable where you are," he said without meeting my eyes. "If I move you to management, we'll lose patients. I need you at that front desk."

I sat stunned. "But you told me I had potential for growth."

"You do," he replied. "Just not here. Not in that way."

That moment taught me a hard truth: my mentor prioritized his own needs over my potential. The lesson stayed with me. From then on, I vowed never to limit someone else's growth to serve my convenience. In my businesses since then, when I see talent, I nurture it—even when I know they may eventually leave. Seven people I mentored have gone on to launch successful companies of their own. Each departure hurt, but each success proved I had learned the dental office lesson: true leadership builds bridges for others, even if it means they might cross beyond you.

THE BIRTHDAY BUDDY TRANSFORMATION

Not every relationship begins smoothly. My colleague—whom I jokingly called my "birthday buddy" because we shared the same birth date—tested my patience from the beginning. Her communication style was blunt, almost abrasive. To me, it felt rude, devoid of the warmth I considered essential.

Our first major clash happened during a client presentation. I had invested hours crafting a trust-centered approach, emphasizing relationship and partnership. Midway through, she cut in, dismissed my approach as inefficient, and presented a stripped-down numbers-only proposal. The client left confused. I left furious.

For months, we battled. I saw stubbornness. She saw weakness. I wanted collaboration. She demanded efficiency. Meetings turned into battlegrounds. The team split into factions, and morale plummeted.

Then one day, in exasperation, she snapped: "You don't understand. Where I come from, softness gets you nowhere."

For reasons I can't explain, I asked, "Then help me understand."

That question shifted everything. She opened up about growing up in Poland with scarce resources. Her family often lacked basic necessities. In that environment, directness wasn't rudeness; it was survival. When you only had one chance to secure food for your family, there was no room for niceties. Efficiency wasn't a preference. It was a necessity.

Hearing her story reframed everything. I began respecting her sharpness, while also sharing my own experiences where empathy had turned deals around or salvaged relationships that numbers alone would have killed. We started adapting to each other. I became sharper, more direct. She softened, adding warmth. We developed a partnership: she reviewed my proposals for efficiency, and I reviewed hers for connection. We became each other's translators.

The results were astounding. Profits rose, customer satisfaction soared, and morale skyrocketed. That colleague became not just a partner but one of my closest advisors. The birthday we once begrudgingly shared became symbolic of a vision we now shared: business as a union of efficiency and empathy. That transformation taught me one of my greatest leadership lessons—difficult relationships often hide the richest opportunities, if we build bridges instead of walls.

WHEN BUSINESS MEETS LIFE AND DEATH

Business decisions can feel crushing, but they are light compared to matters of life and death. I faced those moments while helping my mother and, later, Michael's mother during their final days. Those experiences permanently etched empathy into my leadership.

That perspective guided me when a pregnant colleague planned to return to work just days after giving birth. She insisted she could juggle calls between feedings, lead meetings while recovering, and keep up a full workload. "Women have been doing this forever," she said.

"I need you to hear something," I told her softly. "You're about to become a mother. Your body will need healing. Your baby will need you. And this company will survive if you take the time you need."

She fought me at first. Her eyes filled with frustrated tears. "If I step back, I'll fall behind. Who will do what I do?"

I shared my own story. When my mother suffered a massive stroke, I nearly boarded a plane for a business trip. Michael stopped me. He looked into my eyes and said, "I won't let you go. You need to be with your mom." Two days later, she passed away with me at her side. Had I chosen business over presence, I would have lost those irreplaceable final moments.

"Setting realistic expectations isn't a weakness," I told my colleague. "It's wisdom. Prioritizing your humanity isn't selfish; it's leadership."

She reluctantly took time off, bonded with her son, and returned months later stronger than ever. She thanked me for giving her "permission to be human." Her story later empowered other employees to claim the time they needed during their own life transitions. That ripple effect remains one of my proudest legacies.

THE DESERT TEST

Michael and I once faced a literal desert test. Driving through the desert, our car sputtered to a stop. The gas gauge had malfunctioned, leaving us stranded miles from civilization with no cell service and dangerously rising heat.

The easy response would have been blame—Who missed the warning light? Who chose this route? Instead, we turned toward each other. Michael's upbringing had made him resourceful. My faith steadied me.

Eventually, a road-worn cowboy stopped. He offered to drive one of us twenty-three miles to get gas. Michael went. I stayed with the car, praying and conserving energy. In the first hour, I fought the fear that Michael might never return. The second hour brought reflection. I asked myself, "If I don't make it, what would I regret?"

The answer came clear: "Not helping more people cross their own deserts. Not showing them the precipice isn't the end but the beginning."

Hours later, dehydrated and exhausted, I saw Michael return with the cowboy. Relief washed over me. That desert became my metaphor for resilience: when you give up, you don't just rob yourself. You rob everyone who needs the bridge that only you can build.

THE ROBBINS REVOLUTION

Tony Robbins expanded my understanding of impact. I first saw him speak to 10,000 people, yet he made each feel personally addressed. He shared his own stories of poverty and abuse, showing how those wounds became the foundation for his mission. That vulnerability, combined with power, created a model I have followed.

Michael helped me translate that inspiration into action. From him, I learned that systems don't kill compassion—they scale it. "You can't help everyone without structure," he told me. "But systems without soul are just machines." Together, we discovered that empathy and business acumen aren't rivals. They're allies that, when combined, create sustainable success.

PEOPLE OVER PROFIT—THE LONG GAME

I've built my business on one principle: "Happy and cared-for employees and clients ultimately drive long-term productivity and profits." Choosing people first has always rewarded me—not only in revenue, but in loyalty, creativity, and culture.

The client I gave extra time to later brought us five major accounts. The colleague I took the time to understand transformed our operations. The team member I supported during the crisis became our top performer. Every time I've chosen empathy over short-term efficiency, the long-term return has far exceeded anything I could have predicted.

More importantly, it created something priceless: a culture where people show up whole, innovation thrives, and loyalty grows naturally. That is the real return on choosing people first.

THE BRIDGE BUILDER'S PROMISE

I've stood at those ledges of fear myself, uncertain if the next step meant success or disaster. That's why I do what I do. Not to be a net that catches people, but to be a bridge builder who helps them cross from doubt to confidence, from isolation to connection, from past failures to future possibilities.

Working with VIP Ignite has given me a platform to impact thousands in the entertainment industry, but the principle extends beyond Hollywood. Wherever you lead—whether in business, family, or life—the truth remains: see people's battles, validate their fears, and remind them of their strength.

The hurricane rain has stopped now, but the lesson remains. Storms will always come. But when we build bridges instead of walls, when we choose humanity first, we don't just endure storms. We help others walk through them.

Because here is what I know after years of standing at precipices and building bridges: when you lead with understanding, you don't just change businesses. You change lives. And when you change lives, you create a legacy no storm can wash away.

Be relentless in the pursuit of who you are and who you were created to be. Your purpose isn't only about you; it's about the millions waiting for the bridge only you can build.

About Deneen

Deneen White is a transformational mentor, writer, and visionary leader whose mission is to help people step boldly into the life they were created for. As President of Talent Services for VIP Ignite and Editor-in-Chief of *The Miami News*, she has become a go-to guide for individuals ready to stop shrinking, silence the noise of self-doubt, and rise into their purpose with clarity and strength.

What sets Deneen apart is her ability to see people not as they are, but as they can be. Where others notice potential, she recognizes destiny. She believes in the brilliance within every person long before they see it themselves, and she has built a career helping thousands unlock gifts they once hid, ignored, or underestimated. Her signature blend of grounded truth, unwavering belief, and faith-driven direction has made her one of the most trusted voices in personal growth, performance, and creative leadership.

Deneen's own journey is a testament to renewal. She understands what it feels like to lose your voice—and what it takes to reclaim it. She learned early that the fiercest battles are often internal, waged in the quiet corners of the mind. That understanding fuels her work today. She teaches that real transformation is not accidental; it is intentional. It is spiritual. And it begins when you decide to release the story that limits you and step into the one that liberates you.

In every room she enters, Deneen brings a presence that is both calming and catalytic. People often say that one conversation with her can shift the direction of their lives. She has a rare ability to help people see themselves clearly, shed the fears that keep them small, and take courageous, aligned steps toward a future they once believed was out of reach. Working with Deneen is not passive—it is an invitation to rise.

As a writer, Deneen speaks directly to the heart. Her work challenges readers to examine the beliefs that hold them back, embrace the identities that empower them, and step with conviction into the life they are meant to lead. She writes for the person who knows they are meant for more and is finally ready to claim it.

CHAPTER 10

FROM CHAOS TO CLARITY: HOW REDEFINING EVERYTHING SAVED MY LIFE

BY TRACY PETROVIAK

The tire iron lay three feet from my father's truck. I could see it clearly—the cold metal against the dirt of the racetrack parking lot, just close enough to reach. One clean swing, my mind whispered. *This will work.* My hands were steady. My breathing was calm. What terrified me wasn't the violence in the thought—it was how natural it felt.

Inside the truck, my nine-year-old son was crying, locked in with a man who understood exactly how to terrify a child. That morning, he'd been buzzing with excitement just to drive anything with wheels—the pure, innocent joy my father knew exactly how to weaponize. Now my father was telling him that if he didn't do exactly what he wanted, he'd make sure the state took his baby sister, his half-sister on his dad's side. And he didn't stop there. He told my son he'd have to choose: keep his relationship with me, or lose his race car and the dream he'd been building since he was old enough to wrap his hands around a steering wheel. It wasn't discipline; it was psychological warfare designed to break him and destabilize me.

I walked straight up to the door and told my father he had three seconds to let my son out—or I would rip him through the windshield.

A crowd was forming. That's what stopped me—not morality, not restraint, but the awareness of the trap. My father was a narcissistic sociopath, and manipulation was his art form. He knew how to engineer a scene, provoke a reaction, and then stand in the calm afterward while the person he targeted looked unhinged. If I touched him in public, it wouldn't reveal who he really was—it would validate the image he had spent decades constructing.

So I did the hardest thing I could do: I walked away.

Two days later, in the quiet aftermath of the chaos, I did something even more radical. I took out a notebook and wrote down my definition of what a father should be. It wasn't complicated. Protective. Kind. Supportive. Honest. Someone who puts their child's well-being first.

Then I put my father, Lloyd, next to the list.

He didn't embody a single attribute on that list. Not one. And in that moment, I finally saw the difference between a title someone holds and the truth of who they choose to be.

The pain I'd carried for decades finally made sense. I was suffering not because of who he was, but because I kept trying to force him into a definition he never had the capacity to meet. If he were just a stranger I met on the street, I wouldn't have introduced myself. I certainly wouldn't have handed him access to my child.

That moment cracked something open in me. I realized I could redefine everything: roles, relationships, titles, and even the meanings I had inherited about love, safety, strength, and sanity.

At one point in my childhood, I had eleven sets of grandparents—an ever-shifting roster created by constant divorce and remarriage, not by a big, connected family. Holidays were rotations of fractured loyalties. Six Christmases in two days. Three Thanksgivings where one house hated the people in the house you had just left. You don't build an identity in that environment. You build instincts.

You learn to scan a room before you enter it. You learn to shape-shift. You learn that safety means disappearing into whatever keeps you off someone's target list.

In a world where adults spun in and out like revolving doors, my nervous system learned early that survival depended on staying small, staying quiet, and never doing anything that could be used against me as "crazy."

That's where a hidden definition built itself inside me:
Safety = shifting into the trauma response that keeps other people calm.

As a child, that feels true. It keeps you alive. As an adult, it destroys your life.

You mistake dysfunction for normal. You tolerate what should be intolerable. You stay in situations that bleed you dry because leaving feels like stepping into a hurricane. That's why I stayed in my first marriage far longer than I should have.

Divorce didn't just mean ending a relationship—in my world, divorce equaled crazy. And "crazy" was the identity I had spent my entire life trying to outrun.

That survival program—*don't equal crazy*—had been running long before I knew what it was. And because the unconscious mind doesn't process negatives, all it ever heard was "crazy." The harder I tried not to become it, the faster I ran toward situations that made me look exactly that.

I endured serial infidelity. I collapsed from a size nine to a size zero in six weeks, then manifested three bleeding ulcers in six more. I threw up everything I ate because my body knew what my mind refused to acknowledge: staying was killing me.

When I finally sat across from a therapist—skin gray, body failing—his solution was simple:
"We'll put you on medication so you don't care as much."

I filled the prescription, took one pill, and immediately forced myself to throw it up. Because in that moment, clarity hit me like a freight train.

My mother had spent years on twenty-two different medications. Not healed—managed. Sedated. Diminished. A version of herself that didn't belong to her anymore. I saw that path in front of me, and I knew: swallowing that pill wasn't coping. It was disappearing. He wasn't treating the cause; he was treating the symptom of a definition I had inherited without ever choosing it.

So I chose something else. I chose divorce. And I chose to start asking different questions.

Here's the truth: the unconscious mind is a hard drive. It stores every program, every definition, every emotional loop you absorbed long before you had the ability to question any of it. Most of your operating system was installed between zero and eight years old, when you had no filter and no choice.

Today, I see the same thing in my clients. They spend years in talk therapy, reliving the same stories, activating the same emotional states, walking out of sessions vibrating at the same frequency they came in with. And that frequency keeps old programs alive—especially the skewed definitions of safety, love, worthiness, and identity wired into them during childhood.

The body stays loyal to what it knows, even when what it knows is destroying you.

I went all in trying to understand this. I devoured books. I attended seminars. I studied energy modalities, hypnotherapy, and quantum meditation. I even cohosted a live radio show in the early 2000s where I taught how the unconscious mind operates—how frequency, vibration, and the internal programming you carry determine what you manifest, and why you keep recreating the same emotional reality no matter how hard you try to think differently.

Every modality gave me pieces. None gave me the whole solution. So I built it myself.

I started treating the unconscious mind like a computer. If you have corrupted files (trauma), outdated programs (childhood definitions), and viruses (toxic patterns), you can't just talk about them. You have to clear and rewrite the code using the language the unconscious actually understands.

Most people don't know this: The unconscious mind thinks in pictures. It doesn't process negatives. It doesn't have a sense of humor. It responds to tone, imagery, and the internal movie you're running—not the words coming out of your mouth.

If you say, "I don't want to be sick," the only picture your mind produces is sickness. If you say, "I don't want to be abandoned," your body feels the image of being left. If I say, "Don't think of yellow," you see yellow instantly.

And if it's icy outside and someone says, "Don't slip and fall," your mind flashes an image of you slipping—and then fights not to fulfill it. But if they say, "Walk carefully and stay grounded," your mind creates a completely different picture, and your body follows it.

This is how the unconscious keeps old definitions alive: through the pictures you repeat, the emotions you rehearse, and the tones you internalize without even realizing it.

People talk about the Law of Attraction like it's magic, but it isn't. It's mechanics. Understanding this changed everything—because when you change the picture, you change the emotional signal, and when you change the signal, the entire trajectory of your life begins to shift.

One client learned that as a child, the only time she was nurtured was when she was sick. Her unconscious created a definition: **Sick = loved.** Every time she moved toward health, her protector—the part of her psyche running below conscious awareness—sabotaged her progress, because at a deep level, health meant losing love. Once we cleared that definition, her system finally released the pattern.

The hardest part of this work isn't identifying the programming. It's being willing to lose the people who need you to stay broken.

When my frequency started shifting, I lost relationships—friends, relatives, people who were invested in the version of me that absorbed their chaos so they never had to face their own.

I had been raised to believe that being useful equaled being worthy, that fixing people proved my value, and that overgiving earned belonging. I learned that strength meant how much pain I could absorb without breaking, and that love meant sacrificing myself—even taking on other people's abuse—just to keep them from leaving. Those definitions came from survival, not love.

Years later, my body brought me to my knees again. My body kept collapsing in all the places my identity was asking to evolve.

At twenty-three, doctors told me I had less than a ten percent chance of carrying a child. I carried my son anyway, through a pregnancy that nearly killed me. After an emergency C-section, I spent five hours in surgery and eleven days in the hospital. I left weighing less than I did before I became pregnant. Four days later, I was back with sepsis.

Years later, Lyme disease dragged my husband David and me to the edge again. We were separately infected, then cross-contaminated each other with different strains.

I went from a size five to a size fifteen in ten days as my organs began shutting down.

A doctor looked at my labs and said, "The last patient I saw with blood like yours died in three weeks."

We didn't die.

David spent every waking hour he had, sometimes only a few at a time, researching anything that might keep us alive. He was too sick to work. So I carried the financial load while he fought for our survival. It took four years of clawing our way back.

By June 2019, we had finally made it—the strongest health of our lives, business thriving, hope returning.

Then black mold hit.

By early 2020, we were sick again. When we found the source, I tested at six times the lethal limit. The neurotoxins locked my nervous system into permanent hypervigilance. Spike headaches that took my vision. Auditory distortion that made people's voices sound like Charlie Brown's teacher. Memory lapses that erased my own name.

David did what he had always done in crisis—dove into research, hunting for anything that might keep us alive as the mold dismantled our health.

Recovery wasn't quick. It wasn't linear. It took four years just to get my footing back, and I continue to rebuild layer after layer of my health and nervous system—made possible, once again, by David's determination to keep us alive.

The mold didn't just poison my body—it rewired my system into nonstop hypervigilance. The neurological chaos made me feel like I was unraveling mentally, which accelerated the old program that had always been there: *Don't be crazy. Prove you're sane.* And the more my body malfunctioned, the louder that program became.

I hadn't outrun my programs. I simply couldn't recognize them while my body was in survival mode. Once my system stabilized enough to give me clarity, the patterns became visible. And once something becomes visible, you can finally change it. Seeing that program clearly didn't just free me from it—it returned me to myself.

Here's the part I need you to hear: If you feel stuck—if nothing you've tried has created the shift you need—it has nothing to do with talent, timing, luck, or connections. It has everything to do with definitions.

The beliefs you carry about your worth, your identity, your limits, and your possibilities were programmed into you before you had the capacity to question them. Those definitions run silently, shaping your choices, repeating your patterns, pulling you back into familiar cycles even when you desperately want something different.

You can't mindset your way out of unconscious programming. You can't outthink what was installed emotionally.

You have to go deeper. You have to clear the definition at its root and rewrite the code. When the definition changes, the identity changes. And when the identity changes, your entire reality reorganizes around it.

That's the work I do now—helping people identify the definitions that have been running their lives, clearing the old patterns, and installing new ones that finally match the life they want to create.

I didn't win because I bypassed trauma. I won because I decoded it until the pattern collapsed.

And I'm still decoding. Still integrating. Still discovering new layers. Because relentlessness isn't perfection—it's persistence. It's rising again and again, even when falling feels easier.

Your story isn't over. It's asking you to face the truths that scare you, redefine the meanings that limit you, and choose, moment after moment, to keep going when every part of you wants to stop.

If you're standing at that edge, hear me clearly: The only thing that ends your story is the moment you decide you're done. Until then—be relentless.

About Tracy

Tracy Petroviak is an awareness coach, hypnotherapist, and creator of the I AM Code—work designed to help people remap the unconscious mind and replace trauma-coded definitions with coherent, life-giving ones. Early-life trauma shaped her nervous system; today, she teaches practical ways to recode it into stability and sovereignty. Her approach was forged in real fire: a high-risk pregnancy doctors called impossible; a first marriage that collapsed under betrayal; a years-long battle with Lyme disease; and a black-mold exposure that locked her system into survival mode. Each collapse became initiation. Each initiation became method.

Refusing sedation or resignation, Tracy pursued the science and practice of change with insatiable curiosity. She is certified in Reiki and studied Spiritual Response Therapy, Reconnective Healing, and Hawaiian mysticism—including Hoʻoponopono—with respected teachers, integrating their core principles with cultural respect and practical application. Discovering hypnotherapy gave her a direct pathway to the unconscious—where definitions live, and lasting change takes root. In the early 2000s, she co-hosted *Dynamite Awareness with TNT*, a live radio program exploring quantum manifestation, the unconscious mind, and applied transformation long before they were mainstream. Weekly live teaching demanded rigor; she distilled wide reading into clear tools people could use immediately.

Out of the crucible of illness, Tracy and her husband, David, built Electro Regen Therapy (ERT)—a next-generation PEMF system and education hub that supports recovery, nervous-system regulation, and performance for individuals and clinics across the U.S. While technology plays a role, service sits at the center. Tracy's work weaves somatic awareness, hypnotherapy, and precise language so clients align images, words, and physiology with the outcomes they actually want.

Tracy lives as both practitioner and perpetual student—always decoding, refining, and growing into the truer version of herself. She tests everything she teaches, revisits her own definitions, updates protocols, and integrates new research so clients benefit from living, evolving work. Her philosophy is simple and hard-won:

definitions are destiny. "I didn't win because I avoided trauma," she says. "I won because I kept decoding it until it had nothing left to teach me." Today she guides clients to stabilize their I AM identity, heal protector patterns, and move from survival to sovereignty—without bypassing the truth of their stories.

Explore programs, recordings, and writings at www.IAMCode.co

CHAPTER 11

I AM OKAY: WHEN EVERYTHING WAS BREAKING, I WAS STILL BECOMING

BY GRACIE L. ESCHER

The emergency room lights were too bright at four in the morning. I lay restless on the gurney, wedding dress hanging in the closet at home, while the heart monitor beeped its irregular rhythm. Atrial fibrillation; my heart literally refused to beat normally on the morning I was supposed to marry him. My shoulder throbbed with that familiar exhaustion that made climbing stairs feel like scaling mountains. Upon arriving at the ER, the nurse first administered aspirin, then performed an EKG. I waited for the nurse while she was preparing the two tiny tablets, the medication that would hopefully reset my heart's rhythm before I'd need the paddles.

This was my third emergency room visit since we'd started dating. There would be seven more during that abusive marriage.

As I lay there, listening for my next heartbeat to be in rhythm, the quiet, still spaces in between the beats were where I felt alive. Soothingly, my inner voice reassured me that my children would be okay. I nodded, knowing and feeling this was absolutely true. Then, one more thought, which felt crushing, I never wrote my book.

YOU CAN CHANGE YOUR MIND

I was twenty-eight years old, about to walk into my second marriage wearing a hospital bracelet under my wedding dress, and the universe was literally stopping my heart to get my attention. I went through with the wedding anyway. Sometimes we need to be broken completely before we understand we were never meant to be fixed. We were meant to be free.

THE PERFECT STORM OF CONDITIONING

My story doesn't begin in that emergency room. It began as an innately innocent, hopeful child, born with a very sensitive nature. From society's conditioning to cultural expectations, being the good kid in the caring and very watchful neighbourhood I grew up in, and as my parents were above and beyond kind to others, they taught me to be kind to others too. Those last points I took extremely literally as a little girl. Kindness and making sure I was a good girl translated to me as complying to avoid conflict, extreme people-pleasing, and making myself small. My belief was that keeping the peace was more important than speaking my truth.

Now, years later, and many compromises, I have released any shame or guilt for childhood survival habits. Please don't be hard on yourself, forgive yourself, and when you can, forgive the person who hurt you. Life is too short to continue to live in pain. Choose peace and love always, and make self-love your highest priority by speaking up for yourself.

At the time, because I was missing my inner voice messages, my atrial fibrillation returned, which had disappeared after my first marriage ended. The morning of our wedding, as nurses worked to stabilize my heart rhythm, my body was screaming what my voice couldn't: Don't do this.

THE THEFT OF SELF

Abuse doesn't announce itself with violence. It begins with the slow erosion of your ability to think clearly. Within months of the marriage, I couldn't make a sandwich. I would stand in my own kitchen, paralyzed, thinking: "Where is the bread? How many slices do I need? What goes in a sandwich?" My brain, once sharp enough to get a degree, couldn't sequence the simple steps of lunch preparation.

During both pregnancies, even as my body was being controlled and my mind was being scrambled, I would whisper to my babies: "You speak up for yourself. You use your voice." I was giving them what I couldn't give myself—permission to exist loudly, to take up space, to say no. My first son emerged with this gift intact. He is a high achiever and very well-liked by all. He commanded attention even as a baby simply by existing, drawing servers in restaurants to his light. My second son inherited my gentleness but learned to use it as strength, fist-bumping new players at soccer practice, making everyone feel welcome. A natural leader as well.

But their mother? I was disappearing. The emergency room became familiar territory—seven or eight visits during the marriage, each time my heart literally trying to escape my chest. Lying on those gurneys, I would tell myself my children would be okay if I died. But that thought about the unwritten book haunted me. It wasn't about becoming an author. It was about having a story worth telling, a self worth expressing, a voice that deserved to be heard.

The moment everything changed wasn't dramatic from the outside. Seven years ago, I realized my children were in danger, not just from witnessing their mother's slow dissolution, but from learning that this was what love looked like. The epiphany was quiet but absolute: staying was no longer the safe option. Leaving was the only way to save all three of us.

In the months after leaving the abuse, even the simplest interactions felt overwhelming. The first time I went shopping without my kids, I couldn't respond to a Best Buy associate who asked if I needed help. Years of isolation had stripped away my confidence; I had become so used to second-guessing every word and anticipating the next explosive moment that speaking to another adult felt impossible. That day, four different employees approached me, and each time I froze. I found a charger on my own, hurried through the checkout, and ran to my car. Only once I was safely inside did the tears come. *Why can't I even have a conversation?* And then, a harder question followed: *How do I learn to have one again?*

With my stomach still in knots, I thought about the reps who had asked, "Can I help you find anything?" I made a quiet promise to myself: I would go back—every week if I had to—until I could answer them. On the seventh day, still terrified, I returned. I forced out the words "memory stick," accepted the help, and rushed out the door. But I came back the next week, and the next. By week seven, something shifted. I asked for batteries, added "please," and when the rep handed them to me, I said "thank you" with steady confidence. I walked out of the store smiling—because in that small moment, I had begun to reclaim what the abuse tried to erase: my voice.

THE LEARNING CURVE OF LIBERATION

Freedom, I discovered, is a skill you have to learn. I had spent four decades as a people-pleaser, putting everyone else's feelings first, never saying no, nor having a different opinion, believing that avoiding conflict meant creating peace. Boundaries—a new word for me at forty-four. Teachers, like Dr. Wayne Dyer and Vishen Lakhiani, are where I began understanding that the fear-based living I was conditioned in wasn't my truth.

What was true, I learned, was to trust your gut instincts. Feel them. If your decision doesn't go the way you expected, feel it, learn from it, and then let it go.

The program called "Peace and Power" for abusive relationships provided specialized counseling. My counselor pushed me to my limits, helped me see that protecting my children meant protecting myself first. "You have to press charges if you are mistreated," she insisted. I was too terrified then, but her words planted seeds.

The practical realities were overwhelming. After years as a stay-at-home mom and moving my sons and me out and away from the abuser, I needed employment. My solution? Get my lifeguarding certification back. I'd loved that job since volunteering at twelve, when my parents said I "swam like a fish." But there was a catch: the 400-meter swim requirement. You have to complete it in under ten minutes.

I was fifty and a half years old.

THE RACE THAT CHANGED EVERYTHING

The pool at the lifeguard certification test was divided into lanes. Nine of us were testing, four girls and five boys, all between sixteen and twenty-four years old. The instructor, perhaps thinking he was being kind, placed me with the boys. These kids were ripped, skinny, young, and everything I wasn't. I was fifty and a half years old. For a moment, that familiar panic from my teenage certification tests crept in; it took all my effort to swim 400m in 10 minutes. Then I remembered something my uncle always said about eating "humble pie." I decided to have a different meal.

"Just have fun," I told myself as we lined up at the pool edge. "Be in this moment. Be present. Just go for it."

The instructor called "Go!" and I dove in. The water was exactly where I belonged, where I'd always belonged. First stroke, second stroke, finding my rhythm. Halfway down the first length, I glanced sideways—all four boys were behind me. Not just beside me. Behind me.

"Stay in your happy space," I coached myself. "This feels good. Stroke by stroke."

When I touched the wall at the finish, there was silence. Complete, cricket-chirping silence. I was alone at the wall, the others still swimming. "What's my time?" I gasped out. "What's my time?"

Eight minutes and forty seconds.

Not just under the required ten minutes—I had destroyed it. At fifty years old, I had swum faster than my sixteen-year-old self ever could. I spent the rest of the week walking through the world with an involuntary smile. I was invincible. Not because I had beaten a group of young men in a race, but because I had finally stopped racing against who I thought I was supposed to be.

THE WISDOM OF BECOMING

My sixty-eight-year-old grandmother, who raised fourteen children with everything important stored in her bra, died with a smile on her face. Even in her final moments, she was still giving, still radiating joy despite cancer taking up more and more space in her body. She was my first everyday superhero, showing me that you can carry immense pain and still choose to be the light for others.

Be the lighthouse in your life. You have a choice to show up your best each day. For your most fulfilled life smile, even if it's an invisible one in your heart from a happy memory. I invite you to close your eyes at this moment, smile, and think of a very happy or peaceful time for you. Yes, your happiness and feeling good are just a thought away.

This is what I learned: You can be in the emergency room and choose joy. You can be devastated by betrayal and take your children to the park. You can be afraid and brave. You can be broken and becoming. We don't have to choose one truth. We get to be both.

I learned to replace "I got to" with "I get to." I get to wash dishes because I have food to eat off them. I get to stand at the sink because my body is capable. I get to pick up my children because they exist, and I'm here to do it. This shift from obligation to gratitude changed everything.

Today, I teach swimming to people with extreme water fears. Some of them have nearly drowned, and others have never felt safe in their bodies. I create a space where they can believe in me, believing in them before they take that first step into the pool. I write picture books to help people of all ages learn to read, including seniors who grew up on farms and never had the chance. I'm working on one honoring my grandmother's journey, using her fourteen children to teach numbers and months.

"Sell your cleverness and buy bewilderment."—Rumi

I sold my need to be perfect through exhaustion. I bought the bewilderment of living in awe with a childlike curiosity.

THE RELENTLESS TRUTH

Two days after leaving my marriage, I made a sandwich without thinking about it. Bread, mayo, turkey, cheese, and lettuce all assembled without my brain short-circuiting. It was such a simple thing, but it told me everything: the paralysis wasn't permanent. The fog wasn't me. The confusion was never about my capability, but instead about control.

My parents, now in their seventies, have transformed too. They've learned to let go of their natural desire to protect me. "Gracie, just be you," they say with a smile. My mother and father have found even more love to shine on others, just as their moms, wearing the same radiant, joyful smiles that light up rooms and make everyone feel welcome. Always giving others a sense of belonging.

My mother, father and I talk now more than ever, real conversations; kindness is not a weakness, it is very powerful; and yes, as much as using your voice is necessary and brave, if needed no response, silence is also a profound and wise message of strength, or even if it is two or three breaths in and out making it a long pause before you respond. That's okay. My parents keep evolving, staying young, and inspiring. Watching them continue growing gives me hope that transformation has no expiration date.

If you're standing in your own emergency room—whether literal or metaphorical—with your heart refusing to beat normally, with your body screaming truths your voice can't speak yet, know this: You are okay. Even when you can't make a sandwich. Even when you're fifty and starting over. Even when the only race that matters is the one against your own silence.

The gap between where you are and where you want to be isn't talent or timing; it's the decision to stop trying to fix yourself and start setting yourself free. Your next breath can change everything. Your next stroke can carry you past every younger, stronger competitor. Your next word can be the one that finally tells the truth.

I refused to let abuse write my ending. I refused to let conditioning be my story. I refused to let fear of judgment keep me from that pool, that test, that moment of proving to myself that I could still fly through water like the fish my parents always said I was. Every time I whispered to my babies in the womb to use their voices, I was planting seeds for my own eventual roar. Every emergency room visit was my heart demanding I pay attention. Every moment of paralysis was preparing me for the day I would move with absolute clarity.

Be relentless about your own becoming. Be relentless about honoring the voice that whispers "I never wrote my book" in hospital rooms. Be relentless about teaching your children through your own transformation that speaking up isn't just allowed, it's required.

You can be both broken and beautiful. You can be both afraid and advancing. You can be both fifty years old and just beginning.

You are okay. You have always been okay. You will always be okay.

And sometimes, that's the most relentless truth of all.

About Gracie

Gracie L. Escher is an award-winning author celebrated for her upcoming book, *Fearless, Bold, Free: Breaking the Chains of Abuse*. With a profound commitment to enlightening and empowering others, Gracie has transformed her life experiences into a beacon of hope and resilience. As a single parent, swim coach, and community volunteer, she has a unique ability to ignite and illuminate the hidden dreams within others, encouraging them to rediscover and pursue their passions with renewed enthusiasm.

Gracie's passion for teaching and mentoring spans over thirty years, during which she has impacted countless lives through her work as an English teacher for newcomers, a swim instructor, and a devoted community leader. Her true love, teaching swimming, began in childhood when her own instructors recognized her gift for helping others. Now, she dreams of sharing her childlike eagerness online, empowering people worldwide to overcome fears and dive into the joy of water. Her participation in the *Relentless* project marks a significant milestone in her writing journey, as she continues to design stories that uplift and inspire.

In addition to her dedication to storytelling, Gracie is an active member of Toastmasters International and a participant in Tony Robbins' Mastermind community, where she is building a vibrant online space for real-life happiness and personal growth. Whether she's teaching swimming or designing safe, inspiring spaces for sparking inner desires, Gracie is committed to harmony, helping people carve out time for self-care and make space for what they love. Her life's mission is to help others share their stories, stay true to themselves, and feel peace, gratitude, and happiness in every moment.

When she's not writing or volunteering, Gracie treasures time with her family in Canada, including her cherished boys, loving parents, and beloved pets. She believes in living with a mind-body-spirit balance, capturing captivating sunrises, always with a touch of chocolate nearby.

CHAPTER 12

THE SWING TO RELENTLESS

BY THOMAS WALKER

THE SWING THAT CHANGED EVERYTHING

The ambulance doors were wide open as they lifted the stretcher and pushed my mother in. Swollen beyond recognition, an oxygen mask covered her face, forcing air into her lungs, and a white, bloodstained sheet covered her bruised and battered body. My mom was a beautiful soul, gentle and kind. She didn't deserve the beating from the drunken, abusive hands of my father. The paramedics never looked at me as they closed the doors and drove away. I stood there, alone, tears running down my cheeks. The silence was deafening. My world came crashing down, and nobody said a word to me about it.

I was ten years old, having my Saturday morning swing, after watching Superman on TV. I'd rear back and pump my legs harder and harder until I believed I was flying. But that day, the swing couldn't take me high enough to escape what was coming. At the highest point of my swing, my neighborhood friend, Bobby, ran up and said, "Tommie Lee, you need to go home, your dad is beating up your mom." Little did I know it was my last swing.

Two years later, I walked into my grandparents' living room and froze at the TV as Breaking News scrolled across the screen: Tucson man kills woman in southside boarding house. The camera cut to the police leading my father away in restraints, under arrest for killing his mistress.

As the youngest of my mother's six children, maybe I was too young to understand. Feelings of guilt, shame, and low self-esteem began to hijack our young lives. We weren't just children anymore. We were the children of a wife-abusing murderer. We wore that label like a life sentence. One by one, my siblings fell victim to drugs, alcohol, and other addictive behaviors. I wasn't far behind. The trauma drove us down different paths, but every path ended the same.

THE BREAKING POINT THAT BECAME A NEW BEGINNING

My junior high and high school years were transitional. My grandmother kept me close while my grandfather put tools in my hands. Mama Lucy, the mother of a small Pentecostal church, introduced me to faith. Papa Tommie, an auto mechanic, taught me the value of hard work. Their steady guidance became the foundation of the resilience I carry today.

By my freshman year, Mama Lucy fell ill with diabetes. Refusing amputation, Papa Tommie placed her in a nursing home, where she later passed away. Papa Tommie worked two jobs, leaving me home alone and now without her grounding influence. As a sophomore, I earned the starting quarterback position on the junior varsity football team. Later, I moved to running back, where I excelled. For the first time in my life, I found my own identity. But without Mama Lucy's anchor, I drifted into weed, wine, and wilding out. After going off on a teacher, the school kicked me off the team for the rest of the year. My junior year was an absolute blur. Though I had a decent football season, I never really got back on track.

As a senior, I wasn't just a student anymore. I was a father. One afternoon, I walked into the locker room for practice and found my locker empty. The coach learned I had a child during the summer, and without a conversation, I lost my place on the team. I stood staring at the empty hooks, realizing another door had closed. Where were the adults in my life to help guide or speak up for me? Again, the silence was deafening. At seventeen, the boy in me was gone, forced into manhood before I even knew who I was. I dropped out of school and got a job. Still, I pushed through night school and graduated with my class.

Shortly after graduation, I married my girlfriend. She had the determination to make it work, but I was far from ready. My childhood example of marriage ended in a long hospital stay and a prison sentence. I didn't know what family looked like. Sure enough, I kept drifting, and the marriage was short-lived. My breaking point came in the middle of the night, August 27, 1977. I had been drinking, replaying my failures, searching for a way to fix the mess I had made. I decided to visit her, unannounced, and it did not go well. My father wounds took over, destroying any chance of reconciliation. That night, at twenty-one years old, I made the best, worst decision of my life: I jumped into my car and drove away. Almost a full day later, I arrived in Houston, unannounced, at a friend's house who welcomed me with open arms.

Although down, I was not out. I was relentless. I returned to the faith and work ethic instilled in me. For the next twenty-three years, I worshipped, worked, and prayed as I navigated my way through a good ol' boy network that traditionally was not very accommodating to African Americans, yet I persevered. I fought the good fight of faith. Not only did I excel, but I also met and married my adorable wife, Sherry, who, after thirty-five years, still finds me adorable too.

BUILDING THROUGH THE BREAKING

Not only was she adorable, but she was the closest thing to a saint I had ever known. Her quiet commitment to spiritual things drew me out of the Kingdom of darkness and into the marvelous Kingdom of light. She seemed to know I had yet to become. At first, I followed her to church just to impress, but before long, I was singing in the male chorus. I found myself teaching Sunday school, surrounded by a group of students who inspired me through their growth. Then came the moment that changed everything: The church entrusted me with a youth class. Each week, something inside me came alive as I poured myself into those students. My passion did not go unnoticed. The church formed a search committee for a youth pastor. After several interviews, one candidate turned to the senior pastor and asked the question that silenced the room and turned all eyes on me: "Why are you looking for a youth pastor when you already have one?"

The pastor responded, "Tom, do you want this job?" Without hesitation, I agreed. Although I was already well-established in my industrial sales career, this just felt right.

Many wondered if I had lost my mind by walking away from a solid career, a path that made sense on paper, and accepting a youth pastor position. Family, friends, and colleagues shook their heads in disbelief. But in walking away from what made sense, I found my purpose: to serve students. The roots of my decision were in the struggle of my own story. The silence I carried became my assignment: to be the voice and the advocate I'd never had.

However, even inside the church, the calling wasn't simple. Honestly, I don't think they understood me either. I was thirty-eight years old, too old, in some folks' eyes, to be a youth pastor. Whispers followed me everywhere. "He's got to have an ulterior motive. He's trying to split the church. He's chasing his own ambition." None of it was true, but rumors don't need truth to grow. I served under a cloud of suspicion as intense as fighting through the good ol' boy network, only this time the battle wasn't in boardrooms, it was in the church. I had to learn how to lead within a system that often didn't fully see me. I had to serve faithfully, even when trust was slow to come. I had to push through when my methods were questioned or misunderstood. In those moments, I discovered youth ministry is not about performance or applause. It's not showtime. It's about the hard, unseen work of nurturing lives, one seed at a time. Youth ministry is grow time.

Those fifteen years taught me endurance. I learned how to keep showing up when no one clapped. I discovered that being called doesn't mean being celebrated. Most importantly, I realized faithfulness in the shadows often prepares you for impact in the light.

No part of me ever wanted to be a senior pastor. I still remember the moment I was asked to leave, though it didn't come as a command. It came wrapped in a question: "Are you open to pastoring a church?" The weight of those words hit harder than I could have imagined. My chest tightened, my stomach dropped, gut-punched is too light a phrase. In that moment, every insecurity, every doubt about my place in ministry came rushing to the surface. It felt like rejection, like I had failed the very people and place I had poured myself into. Yet, with time, I came to see what I could not in that instant. It was not rejection, but redirection. God was not pushing me out. He was leading me forward. And of course, I said yes, which became another one of the best, worst decisions I ever made. Worst, because I stepped into a role I never desired. Best, because my King was molding and shaping me, teaching me to lead when trust was scarce, to carry responsibility that stretched me, and to stand firm when the ground beneath me shifted. Scars became stories, proof that even the wrong assignment can serve the right purpose.

THE BLESSING WITHIN THE BREAKING

While trying to blaze a new trail in ministry, my siblings began to pass away. In 2004, I lost my brother Ronnie, and for the next ten years, I served them one at a time, while living with a silent heartache. My sister Joyce, my brother Larry, followed by my eighty-four-year-old mother, Willie Mae, and my sister Kathy. Out of five siblings, my brother Richard and I are survivors. I should have been next, but I wasn't. I kept going. I kept pumping my legs. I was relentless.

As a pastor, everyone expected me to shoulder the weight of final arrangements for each of them. In that season, I learned GRACE is an enabler, and an unexpected challenge presented itself: Ronnie's seven-year-old son, Michael, needed a home. All eyes turned to me, Tommie Lee, the one who got out. What they didn't see was the ten-year-old boy still standing in the street watching EMTs take his mother away. Still filled with unprocessed trauma, I opened my mouth and said, "I'll take him." Exhaustion and fear screamed no, but somewhere deeper, purpose whispered yes. That decision made me more than a pastor handling arrangements. It made me an advocate, a father, and a man standing in the gap. Each funeral marked an ending, but also a beginning, pressing me deeper into purpose. When I said yes to my nephew, who affectionately calls me dad, I wasn't just burying my brother. I was redeeming my childhood silence.

As fate would have it, my senior assignment landed me in the hood, at a small church wedged between an elementary and middle school. Serving there became fundamental to the burden I carry today: addressing the absence of transformative discipleship within the local church and repairing the broken connection between the church and its community. I also began to process the difference between a Church Christian and a Kingdom Christian. One goes to church, but the other becomes the church, living out God's reign daily beyond the sanctuary.

I began building relationships in the community. I met folks who had been there for decades. Community elders, young families, single parents, and children who lived from pillar to post, left to fend for themselves. I soon realized all they wanted was for someone to see them. One day, my brother Larry and I were talking when he asked where I pastored. I proudly told him, "In the *hood*, just like where we grew up." He stopped me cold: "Tom, we didn't grow up in the hood. We grew up in a neighborhood where we looked out for one another."

My nine years serving as senior pastor gave me a firsthand account of the challenges our communities face. The effects of systemic oppression, underperforming schools, and gentrification have shackled our communities beyond measure. Many of our churches have aged out and lost their capacity to make a difference. We now have an epidemic of urban, underground, survival theology shaping the character of our youth and community.

Many who got out vowed never to return, not even to serve. However, I am committed to reintroducing the true meaning of the Lord's Prayer: 'Thy will be done on earth as it is in heaven,' a statement of alignment, back into our neighborhoods by raising kingdom-minded students to lead the way. But I'm not doing it alone. Students I served more than twenty-five years ago are now leading the way. They are young, successful professionals who recall a time when someone refused to give up on them.

THE DECISION THAT CHANGES EVERYTHING

Through all of life's unexpected turns, I'm still swinging. My journey of resilience led me to found TOUCH Kingdom Outreach (TKO). Our vision is to ignite a generation of leaders who rise from brokenness to brilliance. We are committed to restoring dignity, awakening purpose, and advancing the Kingdom in every area of life. We envision transformed communities where people not only live well and finish well but also leave legacies that outlive them. If you got out, come back. Let's utilize those empty church buildings to educate our children and put the Neighbor back in Hood.

YOUR MOVE TOWARD RELENTLESS

If you're in the messy middle right now, experiencing financial strain, family drama, or career uncertainty, I need you to hear this: The gap between where you are and where you want to be isn't about talent or timing. It's tenacity. Here's what I'm asking you to do tonight: Write down one thing from your past that feels like it's disqualifying you from your future. Tomorrow, take one action to flip that script. If addiction runs in your family, volunteer at a recovery center. If poverty marked your childhood, mentor a child who's there now. If rejection defines you, become the person who includes others. Your setback is someone else's comeback waiting to happen. But only if you decide to be relentless about transforming it.

I'm still rearing back, pumping my legs, rising higher, and refusing to quit. My earthly father won't define my legacy or that of my sons, grandsons, and great-grandsons. Every morning, I wake up and make the same decision: Live well. Finish well. Be relentless.

Setbacks don't define you; your next decision does. GRACE is your enabler: be Grateful, be Resourceful, be Authentic, be Committed, be Excellent.

The swing is waiting. Your legs are strong enough. Rear back and pump as hard as you can!

Be relentless.

About Thomas

Thomas Walker is a retired pastor with twenty-five years of faithful Kingdom service. He earned his B.A. in Leadership from the College of Biblical Studies in Houston, Texas, and later graduated from the Perkins School of Theology's Course of Study program. Thomas is also a proud alumnus of the DeVos Urban Leadership Initiative (DVULI), a nationally-respected program dedicated to developing emerging urban youth leaders.

Before entering full-time ministry, Thomas enjoyed a successful twenty-three year career in Industrial Sales. After experiencing significant professional achievement, he surrendered to a deeper calling—serving the next generation. He transitioned into student ministry, where he spent fifteen years cultivating a legacy of transformational discipleship in the lives of students throughout Houston (receipts available upon request).

Thomas then served ten years as senior pastor in Houston's historic 3rd and 5th Wards, where he developed a profound commitment to urban ministry, community empowerment, and the spiritual formation of underserved neighborhoods. His mission is clear and compelling: to Put the Neighbor back in Hood.

At sixty-five years young, Thomas boldly enrolled at Dallas Theological Seminary to pursue his master's degree in biblical and theological studies, demonstrating his belief that learning, growth, and purpose have no expiration date.

A certified Life Coach, Thomas identifies himself as an ATTM—Author, Teacher, Transformational and Motivational Speaker. His message blends Kingdom truth, personal development, and lived experience, empowering people from all walks of life to rise, reign, and take dominion over their personal territory.

His personal motto anchors every aspect of his work:
Live well. Finish well. And have a GRACE Day, one day at a time.
Be Grateful. Resourceful. Authentic. Committed. And whatever you commit to, execute.

Website: tkoutreach.org
Email: tw@tkoutreach.org

CHAPTER 13

RELENTLESSLY SEEKING YOUR TRUTH: WHEN INTUITION DEMANDS YOU BECOME WHO YOU'RE MEANT TO BE

BY PEGGY EBRING

The black hole gaped before me—a dark mouth slowly swallowing my father's coffin inch by inch. January 2012. Trois-Rivières cemetery, Guadeloupe. The tropical sun beat down mercilessly, but I felt only cold. Two weeks earlier, he'd been celebrating Christmas, laughing over rum punch, playing pétanque with his friends, his hands steady as always when he threw the silver ball. Now this awful box contained everything that remained. The polished wood gleamed obscenely in the bright Caribbean light.

I stood there devastated, my legs threatening to buckle, dissolving into grief so complete I didn't know if I would ever recover. The mourners around me blurred into shadow. Their words of comfort fell like stones into an endless void. With every inch the coffin sank, a part of me died too. My heart, ravaged and raw, descended with him into that abyss.

Then, in that moment of purest agony, a question pierced through my chaos: "What is life?"

I frowned, confused by its appearance, its timing. Why now? Why this? The question wouldn't leave. It spun in my mind like an obsession until suddenly, like a flash of divine clarity, everything shifted. One small pronoun changed my entire destiny.

The real question wasn't "What is life?" It was "What is *My* life?"

I froze. I had no idea. What was my mission? Why was I here? Who was I, really? So many questions. Not a single answer.

Standing at my father's grave, I made the only decision that made sense: I would find those answers at all costs. I swore a sacred oath that I would discover my life's mission and make a positive impact, even though I had no idea how. That divine pact would push me deeper into myself than I'd ever dared go. It would demand I become relentless about my truth.

THE VOICE THAT WOULDN'T BE SILENCED

The following year after that cemetery moment, I searched desperately for answers. Then my intuition started sending me clues. The first one was a hint about natural medicine. I pulled the thread and ended up training as a naturopath, despite my then-husband's protests about the low pay. I left my meaningless investment banking career—the one I'd chosen by default, not desire, the one that had me staring at risk management softwares while my soul withered. I also became an intuitive life coach. Then my intuition started showing me unexpected, senseless, crazy images. During meditations, I kept seeing a book. Not reading one—writing one. The message was persistent, relentless: Write.

Impossible. I wasn't a writer. I'd never kept a diary. Even birthday cards left me uncomfortable, staring at a blank space. My French literature marks in school had been abysmal—eight or nine out of twenty, consistently. Red ink bled all over my papers. Teachers wrote powerlessly. "Needs improvement." The structured system hadn't been adapted to my creativity, though I didn't know that then. I only knew I wasn't good with words. Words were for other people—literary people, creative people, real writers, not for rational scientific minds.

My logical mind battled my intuition for months. Write a book? Me? The girl who'd been so painfully shy she couldn't even say "stop" to a bus driver? The girl who was so often lost for words? The woman whose ego had developed an elaborate strategy to keep her quiet and invisible?

But intuition is relentless when you've made a pact with your truth.

WHEN YOUR EGO FIGHTS YOUR CALLING

Finally, after months of inner struggle, I opened just a crack to the possibility. Sometimes life is simply waiting for you to say yes—even a fearful yes, a small yes, a doubtful yes—before it can start unfolding.

The coaching company I had trained with, Natural Success Academy, offered an intuitive writing course with William Whitecloud. I flew to Mozambique, both hopeful and doubtful, not fully believing there was a book in me. After the first training, I came back home and saw myself frozen at the blank page after writing a few pages. The intuitive writing process required me to become a channel, to trust something beyond my logical mind. It meant sitting with blank pages and allowing words to come through me, not from me. Although I had no rules to unlearn, no literary pretensions to shed, my ego found endless ways to stop me. I had to take the course twice because my resistance to writing was so fierce.

I kept *forgetting* about the book. Days would pass, then weeks. I had to put fluorescent Post-it Notes everywhere—on my wall, my computer, even in my bathroom. "WRITE," they screamed. Then came the excuses: "If I don't have two hours, it's not worth it. I won't have enough time to get in the flow." My intuition countered: Write anyway. Half an hour. One paragraph.

The fear of humiliation haunted every sentence. This sucks, my mind would scream. You'll be publicly humiliated. Everyone will see you're a fraud. For two and a half years, I battled these voices.

My burning desire to live my true nature and purpose kept me going. My deep knowing is that if intuition gives you a vision, a way already exists to make it real. I didn't trust myself to write, but I trusted divine guidance to show me my truth.

THE DAY EVERYTHING CHANGED

The most devastating attack came the morning of my first TV appearance. After years of invisible work, years of small coaching sessions in quiet rooms, I'd finally been invited to host a segment on Coach Privé, a show on Martinique La Première television. This wasn't just any appearance—this was my emergence from hiding, my declaration to the world that I had something worth saying. The night before, excitement and terror battled in my chest, despite the fact that I had been practicing for days. This was everything I'd dreamed of. This was everything I'd feared.

I slept poorly, worrying I would not be good enough. I woke officially at 6 a.m. We were filming at 9 a.m. I opened my mouth to practice one more time.

My voice was completely gone.

Not weak. Gone. Like someone had reached into my throat and stolen it in the night.

Panic flooded through me, ice-cold and paralyzing. My hand reached for the phone to cancel. This was the universe telling me I wasn't ready. Then intuition flashed through the panic like lightning: "Wait. This is too strange. See what's really happening."

Everything related to voice and verbal expression carries deep meaning for me. At nine years old, I'd dared to be a leader in a playground game. I fell, breaking my two front teeth. I got painfully reminded of my egoic rules. My child's mind internalized a devastating message: Being visible leads to pain. Leading brings disaster. Better to stay quiet and small to stay safe. After, I slipped into the smothering and suffocating shadows of myself.

That morning, decades later, my ego was using the same old strategy. Being seen by thousands of viewers? Speaking my truth publicly? Too dangerous. Solution: Shut her up. Steal her voice.

I realized this loss of voice was an illusion—a protective mechanism, not a physical reality. I decided to take back my power.

I affirmed that my voice would return and we would film as planned. I talked to my body. I connected with my inner child, assuring her we were safe now.

I practiced energy healing, drank herbal tea, and refused to accept my ego's version of reality.

My voice returned just in time.

That experience taught me about the power of aligned choice—standing in your truth no matter the external circumstances. No matter what is happening, choose alignment with your inner truth.

FROM TERROR TO TRIUMPH

Each time I said yes to my truth despite fear, miracles appeared. When intuition prompted me to direct a short film at a Kinomada event—despite having zero filmmaking experience and being scared—I dared to raise my hand. Using my intuitive process, I developed a modern take on Little Red Riding Hood where the forest was the mind, and the wolf represented our egoic limiting beliefs.

Turning that vision into a script was a four-day nightmare. I'd never even seen a script before. But magic happened. When I needed support, the right people showed up. The filmmaker Junsunn Lo rescued me, and we co-wrote the script. When we needed a wolf head prop, a woman appeared whose partner made theatrical costumes. The film "Abysse" was born from pure trust in the process.

When intuition showed me visions of Pawol Fanm ("Women's Voices"), an event celebrating creative and inspiring women committed to making a positive impact, I got inspired and shit scared. Me? Organize an event? I had no money—my bank account was nearly empty. I had no experience—I'd never organized anything bigger than a dinner party. My organizational skills were terrible—I routinely forgot things, and my desk is like a war zone. Time management was my nemesis.

But the vision wouldn't leave me alone. I saw it clearly: women sharing their stories, their struggles, their triumphs. A safe space for silenced voices. Just like mine had been for so long. An invitation to be bold and to dare to follow your truth.

The second edition's vision was even bigger, even more impossible—talks with inspirational women in cinema and television, intimate interviews with pioneering women, an elegant cocktail reception, and documentary screenings in an actual movie theater. The venues alone would cost thousands of euros I didn't have. Still no money. Costs are even higher. My logical mind screamed this was insane.

So I did what any reasonable person would do: I booked the cinema without knowing how I'd pay for it.

I attended Tony Robbins' Unleash the Power Within online, breaking a wooden board to shatter my fears and prove they were an illusion. I worked through course after course on abundance blocks, excavating every limiting belief about money I'd inherited from generations of struggle. I launched a crowdfunding campaign, my hands shaking as I hit *publish*, doubting I could raise enough money.

Then miracles started appearing. The universe responded in ways I never imagined: a venue offered its space for free. Volunteers materialized—women who believed in the vision and wanted to help. A professional journalist I'd never met offered to MC the entire event without payment. She felt we needed more events like mine and wanted to help.

When our chosen documentary was selected by a major local festival—threatening our ticket sales—I used Tony's priming process to raise my vibration and seek solutions. We ended up with an even better film, hosting its Martinique premiere. Every obstacle became an opportunity to practice relentlessness with my truth, to grow in faith.

THE TRUTH LIVES IN THE UNKNOWN

Writing *The Quest* took two and a half years of showing up despite resistance. Two and a half years of battling voices that said I was wasting my time, sometimes writing one sentence in an hour, sometimes deleting everything. But I kept showing up. Again and again. One more day. One more page. One more paragraph.

Creating Pawol Fanm shattered many limiting beliefs about money and worthiness. It forced me to ask for help—something that felt like death to someone who'd learned she's alone and had to manage on her own. It pushed me to step up and let go of the belief that visibility meant pain. It demanded I step into leadership when every cell in my body remembered that nine-year-old girl with broken teeth.

Directing Abysse demanded I trust beyond logic. When the script wasn't coming together, I had to hold on, to trust the Universe would see me through. It always did.

Each challenge was an initiation. Life asking: "How badly do you want to live your truth? What will you face to become who you really are? What will you be willing to let go of to live your true nature and purpose?"

THE POWER OF RELENTLESS TRUTH

The mindset that carried me through? Three core beliefs:

- The Universe is for me. Everything serves my highest good.
- Truth is empowering and liberating when it is embraced.
- I have come here for a reason. I have a purpose. And I will fulfill it.

The truth of who we are lives in the unknown—in those terrifying and thrilling projects that make no logical sense. It's there we meet our deepest fears, release the lies we've believed, and allow our truth to shine.

Today, as a speaker and writer, I help others find the courage to follow their own relentless truth. Every time someone tells me my work inspired and helped them find their true voice, I remember that nine-year-old girl with broken teeth who thought being visible meant being hurt. I remember that morning, my voice disappeared. I remember choosing truth anyway.

YOUR TRUTH IS WAITING

If you're standing at your own black hole moment—grieving who you were, terrified of who you're becoming—know this: A breakdown is simply the breaking of a limiting shell, allowing more light to come through. You are not alone. Divine support surrounds you, even when you can't feel it. You are not your thoughts or your fears. You are not your past. Your past is merely the setup for your brilliance, light, and purpose to be revealed.

That question that found me at my father's grave—"What is MY life?"—it's really asking: Will you be relentless enough to live your truth? Will you keep showing up when your voice disappears, when the money isn't there, when everyone thinks you've lost your mind? Will you trust that whisper of intuition over the roar of fear?

Here's what I know now, what I couldn't have known standing at that cemetery: Your intuition already knows the answer. It's been whispering it all along, despite every fear, every doubt, every logical reason to quit. The gap between where you are and where you want to be isn't talent or timing or luck. It's not about having it all before you start, being ready, or having enough resources.

It's tenacity. It's choosing your truth one more time. And then again. And again. It's being relentless about becoming who you really are, even when that person seems impossible, even when the only thing you have is a stubborn refusal to accept anything less than your truth.

Your next decision can change everything. Not next year's decision. Not next month's. The one you make right now, reading these words.

Dare to say yes to your truth. Even a fearful yes. Even a small yes. Even a doubtful yes. Even a "this-is-crazy-but-I'm-doing-it-anyway" yes.

The universe is waiting to conspire in your favor. But first, you must conspire with yourself. You must become relentless about your own becoming.

Be relentless.

About Peggy

Peggy Ebring is a bestselling author and inspirational speaker who helps women reconnect with their authentic voice and step boldly into their true purpose.

After several years in the high-pressure world of investment banking in London, Peggy experienced a profound spiritual awakening that led her to leave corporate life behind and dedicate herself to truth, healing, and self-expression.

Her journey gave birth to a powerful collection of personal development books—including *The Quest* trilogy—that have inspired thousands of readers. Her writing guides women to heal emotional wounds, release limiting beliefs, and listen deeply to the quiet inner voice that reveals who they truly are.

As a speaker and facilitator, Peggy brings her soul wisdom to diverse platforms. She previously hosted personal development segments on *Ti Tak Forme* and *Coach Privé* for Martinique La Première TV, and currently hosts a monthly segment on Martinique La Première radio. She also leads transformational talks and workshops that empower people to live authentically and courageously.

Peggy is the founder of PAWOL FANM, a vibrant annual event that celebrates and amplifies the voices of inspiring women.

Whether through her books, her voice, or her events, Peggy is devoted to helping women reclaim their inner light, speak their truth, and live a life aligned with freedom, love, and purpose.

CHAPTER 14

WATCH ME: WHEN A STOMA BAG COULDN'T STOP A MARATHON DREAM

BY LISA HORAN

At twenty-two, I woke up from what was supposed to be a routine reversal surgery with two stoma bags instead of one. The reversal had failed in ways the surgeons hadn't anticipated. Catastrophic infection set in immediately. Septicemia, a blood poisoning that kills quickly if untreated, was destroying my body from the inside. A ventilator was breathing for me in intensive care. The doctors prepared my mother for the worst: her daughter might not make it through the night. I endured three surgeries in three weeks. Machines kept me alive while my mother sat beside my bed, watching her daughter slip away and return, slip away and return.

Twenty years later, I crossed the finish line of the London Marathon.

Between those two moments stretches a story about the difference between surviving and living; a distinction I learned costs everything to understand and even more to act upon. This isn't a story about overcoming disability, though I live with a permanent stoma bag. It's not about medical miracles, though I've defied plenty of medical predictions. This is a story about what happens when you stop accepting other people's limitations as your own.

The marathon wasn't my first impossible thing. By the time I stood at that starting line in October 2021, I'd already spent decades proving that the girl who nearly died had more fight in her than anyone imagined. But the marathon was different. It was public. Undeniable. Eight and a half hours of refusing to quit, broadcast for the world to see.

"You know it's 26.2 miles, right?" my in-laws had asked during training, as if I might have confused it with a casual stroll around the park. Their skepticism joined a chorus I'd been hearing for twenty years: *Should you be doing that? Is this safe for someone like you? Haven't you been through enough?*

Here's what I've learned about being told you can't do something: it's the most powerful fuel that exists, if you know how to use it.

THE BREAKING POINT THAT BECAME A BEGINNING

December 2000. A surgeon stood beside my hospital bed explaining that without emergency surgery, I would die. Crohn's disease had created an ulcer on my bowel that could burst at any moment. "We'll take a portion of your bowel, sit it on your stomach, and you'll go to the toilet in a bag," he said, his tone clinical, matter-of-fact.

I'd never heard of a stoma bag. At twenty-one, I barely understood what was happening to my body, but I understood "die" clearly enough. I signed the consent forms.

Waking up with an ileostomy bag attached to my stomach felt like waking up in someone else's life. They promised it would be temporary; just a year, maybe less. I clung to that promise through the awkward adjustments, the leaks, the stares, the shame. One year, then back to normal.

A year later, I went into reversal surgery filled with hope. Finally, I'd get my body back. Finally, I'd be "fixed." I came out with two bags instead of one.

When I finally stabilised, when the immediate threat passed, the surgeons explained my new reality: I would be left with one of the stoma bags permanently. This wasn't temporary anymore… this was my body now.

The depression that followed was a different kind of dying. For years after those surgeries, I existed rather than lived. Worked at a supermarket. Paid my mortgage. Went through the motions of a life that felt like it belonged to someone else. I let other people's concern for my fragility become my own truth. Every suggestion of adventure, every possibility of more, filtered through the same worried questions: "Should you be doing that? Are you sure that's safe?"

The subtext was always clear: *Be grateful you're alive. Don't push it.*

But gratitude without growth is just another cage, and I was slowly suffocating in mine.

WHEN DEATH TEACHES YOU TO LIVE

In 2008, everything changed with a phone call. My close friend had died suddenly from an asthma attack. One day, she was here, laughing, planning, and living. The next, gone. No warning. No time to do the things she'd been saving for someday.

Standing at her funeral, something inside me snapped awake. I was twenty-eight years old and had been sleepwalking since my surgeries six years earlier. Playing it safe. Staying small. Wasting the life I'd fought so hard to keep.

That same year, I quit my full-time job. Everyone said I was crazy to leave security. "You have a mortgage," they reminded me. "You can't just walk away from stability." But stability is an illusion when you've already almost died twice, when you've watched someone younger than you leave this world midsentence.

I got a part-time job at a cinema and went back to college. Not because I had some grand plan, but because I was done just existing. Done letting my scars define my limits. Done living like I was made of glass.

My friend's death had lit a fire under my life. It made me more honest, more urgent, and more alive. Every loss since has only stoked that fire higher. In 2023, I lost my aunty to motor neurone disease. Her body slowly stopped responding to her commands. Before she died, I made sure to thank her for everything, to tell her exactly how much she meant to me. That love, that grief, now fuels my determination to live loudly, boldly, without apology.

Because here's what death teaches you if you're paying attention: someday isn't a day of the week. The things you're waiting to do, the person you're waiting to become, the life you're waiting to live, none of it is guaranteed. We get this moment. This choice. This is a chance to be more than our worst day.

THE IMPOSSIBLE MARATHON

During the 2020 lockdown, something possessed me to apply for the London Marathon. Maybe it was turning forty and realising I was still treating myself like that frightened twenty-one-year-old in the hospital. Maybe it was the global reminder of how quickly everything can change. When I received the acceptance email, I stared at it in shock.

I didn't run. Had never run. Couldn't remember the last time I'd even tried.

I went from couch to marathon in less than six months. It's not that I gave myself that time. It was less than eight months until the marathon when I got the acceptance email. Then, in true Lisa style, I put off starting to train for a couple of months. My goal was insane by any standard, borderline impossible given my starting point. The first training run lasted only minutes before I collapsed, gasping, certain I'd made a terrible mistake. My stoma bag complicated everything. Constant adjustments, backup supplies, and strategic planning for every route. Some days they leaked midrun, and I'd have to find my way home, humiliated and furious.

Training meant morning alarms in British winter darkness, rain that felt personal, and wind that seemed determined to push me backward. My body screamed in protest, but my mind was worse, constantly listing reasons to quit: *You're not a runner. You have a physical disability. You've been through enough. No one expects this from you.*

That last whisper nearly broke me. No one expected this from me. I could quit, and everyone would understand. They'd pat me on the head, tell me I tried, remind me that, considering my "condition," even attempting it was brave.

But I didn't want participation trophies for the damaged. I wanted to cross that finish line.

The day I collapsed at my mother's house during training—bright red, crying, barely able to stand—she looked at me with that specific fear only mothers carry. "This is why I'm worried," she said. She'd seen me at my worst, machines breathing for me, odds against me. Now I was voluntarily putting myself through this.

But something had shifted in my mind. Once I'd decided I was doing this marathon, that was it. The decision was made. In my mind, I'd already finished it. I knew with absolute certainty that I would cross that line, even if I had to crawl.

You see, I've been stubborn since birth. My mother tells the story of nurses trying to force-feed me a bottle as a baby. I took it, then promptly threw up all over the nurse who tried to make me take it. When someone tells me I can't do something, something ancient in me burns to prove them wrong. Call it spite motivation if you want. I call it rocket fuel.

EIGHT AND A HALF HOURS OF RELENTLESS

Race day, October 2021. Standing in that crowd of runners, everyone else looked like they belonged. Lean. Athletic. Confident. I was terrified of the bag leaking, of collapsing, of proving everyone right who said I shouldn't be there.

Mile one felt good. Mile five, still strong. By mile ten, something profound shifted. I realised I was actually doing this. Not because I was fast or naturally athletic, but because I'd already decided I would. I made the decision months ago when I got the email to say I was in. When I hit submit on that application, I didn't really think I would get a place. Everything since then was just following through.

The middle miles were hell. Everything hurt. My legs, my back, places I didn't know could hurt. Other runners passed me in waves. People dressed in costume even passed me, including a rhino, an ovary, and a fireman in full uniform, including the large metal oxygen tank. I didn't care. This wasn't about them. This was about me and the finish line I'd already crossed in my mind a thousand times.

Doubt whispered for exactly one second. My body remembered the failure of collapsing at my mother's house during training. My mind remembered the doubt in everyone's eyes. Then I kept going. Because that's what relentless looks like: not the absence of doubt, but moving forward anyway.

Eight and a half hours. That's how long it took me to finish the London Marathon. Eight and a half hours of refusing to quit. Eight and a half hours of proving that determination matters more than natural ability. Eight and a half hours of showing everyone, including myself, what's possible when you decide something is happening, no matter what.

When I crossed that finish line, I wasn't just completing a race. I was rewriting my entire story. The girl with a stoma bag, who nearly died at twenty-two, who everyone thought should just be grateful to be alive, had just done something most healthy people never attempt.

Since that marathon, I've abseiled down buildings despite being terrified of heights. I've been wing-walking on a plane, strapped to the wings while it flew through the sky. I've run multiple half-marathons. Not because I'm special, but because I'm relentless. Not because I'm fearless, but because I've learned that fear is just information, not instruction.

YOUR LIMITATIONS ARE NEGOTIABLE

Twenty-five years of medical trauma didn't make me fragile. It made me unbreakable. Every surgery, every complication, every moment I survived when the odds were against me—that's proof of strength, not weakness. The scars on my stomach aren't signs of damage. They are evidence that I'm stronger than what tried to destroy me.

When people ask why I do these extreme challenges, the answer is simple: Because I can. Because my friend who died in 2008 can't. My aunty showed me what it really means to lose choice. Because someday I won't be able to. And because every single day above ground is a day to prove that surviving isn't the same as living.

If you're standing at your own breaking point—medical, financial, professional, personal—I need you to hear this: You're not too broken. You're not too late. You're not too far gone. You've survived 100 percent of your worst days so far. That's not luck, that's strength. The same strength that got you through will get you beyond.

Different doesn't mean less capable. Surviving doesn't mean settling. And having limitations doesn't mean accepting them as permanent. Your limitations are negotiable. The middle is meant to be messy. Other people's fear isn't your responsibility. And sometimes, spite motivation is the best motivation.

Whatever mountain you're facing, the business you want to start, the goal that seems impossible, the comeback everyone says you can't make, remember this: The only person who needs to believe you can do it is you. Once you truly believe it, once you decide it's happening, the rest is just time and effort.

When the world says you shouldn't, when logic says you can't, when everyone would understand if you quit, you have a choice. You can accept their limitations as your own, or you can say two words that changed everything for me: Watch me.

The gap between where you are and where you want to be isn't talent or timing; it's tenacity. Your next decision can change everything. Your story isn't over. Your setbacks don't define you. Your next decision does.

Don't wait for someday. Don't wait for permission. Don't wait to feel ready. Don't wait for the fear to go away. Just decide. Then be relentless about that decision.

And when they say you can't, when they list all the logical reasons why it's impossible, show them what relentless really looks like.

Watch me became my battle cry. Now it's yours.

About Lisa

Lisa Horan knows what it means to fight for her life and to choose to live it fully. At just twenty-one years old, she faced the unthinkable when Crohn's disease led to major surgeries that left her with a stoma. It was a time of fear, pain, and uncertainty, when simply surviving seemed like the greatest challenge of all. Yet rather than letting that moment define her, Lisa decided it would become the foundation for a life lived with courage, resilience, and relentless determination.

Her journey since has been anything but ordinary. After years of setbacks, surgeries, and struggles with mental health, Lisa chose to embrace life's challenges as opportunities. In 2021, at the age of forty-one, she went from couch to marathon in less than six months, crossing the finish line of the London Marathon against all odds. People doubted she could do it, and some even feared she would harm herself trying. But Lisa proved them wrong, showing that the human spirit is far stronger than any obstacle placed in its way.

Her adventures haven't stopped there. From wing walking thousands of feet in the air, to abseiling, Lisa has made it her mission to do the very things many once said she shouldn't. Each challenge has become a declaration of strength, a statement that adversity does not mean the end of possibility. Her motto, "Watch me!", perfectly captures this attitude, bold, unapologetic, and full of fire.

But Lisa's story is not just about thrill-seeking. It is about survival, about choosing hope when despair seemed easier, and about finding purpose after deep loss. She has faced heartbreak, grief, and the darkest days of depression, yet through it all, she has discovered not only her own strength but the power of sharing her story so that others might find theirs too.

Today, Lisa is a writer, speaker, and storyteller who inspires people to face their own struggles with courage, to chase the adventures that call to them, and to believe that life after adversity can be extraordinary.

You can connect with Lisa at: lisa.author.speaker@gmail.com

CHAPTER 15

THE DAY I REFUSED TO LET MISERY WIN: CHOOSING FREEDOM OVER FEAR AT FIFTY

BY K. LOWERY MOORE

The email notification popped up on my screen at 4:16 p.m. on a Friday afternoon in February. "Voluntary Early Retirement Authority (VERA) Opportunity—Limited Time Offer." My hands trembled as I read it again. Thirty-three years of federal service, and here it was, the escape hatch I'd been praying for since I attended a mid-career seminar almost two decades ago. From the age of thirty-five, I dreamed of being able to take early retirement at fifty, if it was ever offered. I had the years, not the age. Everyone would think I was crazy volunteering to leave the GS-14 position that I fought hard for, but in my soul, I knew it was time. I had sixty days to make a major life decision. My inner voice (or critic) echoed in my head: "You only have four more years to go to reach the minimum retirement age, full benefits (for those with thirty-plus years). Don't leave money on the table... you're almost there. Don't be foolish."

But foolish? I'd been dying a slow death in that cubicle for years, letting someone else's power plays steal my peace, my creativity, my very essence. The supervisor who'd moved me to a smaller cubicle in front of the office, which was a daily reminder that I wasn't the *yes person* they wanted. The exhaustion that hit me every evening was like I'd been in a physical battle. The way my resentment had started seeping into every corner of my life, cluttering not just my house but my soul.

I clicked *Accept*.

My relationship with refusing to quit started when I was ten years old. That's when my mother died suddenly in 1983, leaving me with a grief so heavy that no one in my family knew how to help me carry it. They fed me, clothed me, kept a roof over my head—but nobody taught me how to navigate the darkness. The family carried on as if nothing had happened, as if a ten-year-old could simply adjust to her mother vanishing from existence. So, I learned to create my own safe places. First through rap songs scribbled in notebooks during lunch breaks, then poetry that bled onto pages late at night, eventually novels that gave voice to pain I couldn't speak aloud.

At twenty-two, I wrote a rap song called "That's Life," pouring out my vision to help solve the world's struggles. But with a one-year-old son depending on me, I tucked those dreams away and focused on survival.

By twenty-four, I was a single Black mother with two sons, defying every statistic society had written for me. The media said I should be on welfare. The whispers from family that I was moving too fast. The world expected me to fail. Instead, I was a permanent federal employee at nineteen with my own apartment in Suitland, Maryland, right outside of my hometown of Washington, DC. The pride I felt signing that lease—my name, my space, my independence—was intoxicating. I bought my first house at thirty-two, completed my degree in business administration, and put my boys in private school.

But here's what they don't tell you about beating the odds: sometimes the biggest battle isn't with society's expectations—it's with the exhaustion of constantly proving them wrong. Every achievement felt like a defense, every success a rebuttal to an argument I never asked to be part of.

I remember the day my teenage son called me from our neighborhood in a townhouse community, police lights flashing behind him. "Mom, they need you to confirm I live here." The crack in his voice broke something in me. All those years in private school, all that shelter I'd tried to build around them, and still, the world demanded they prove their right to exist in spaces we'd earned.

I taught them to keep improving, keep pushing, but inside, I was crumbling under the weight of constantly fighting battles on every front.

A pivotal moment for my writing journey and my life was in 2006… stepping on stage at an open-mic night and reciting a poem in memory of my mother. It was the fulfillment that I missed. That courage led to eventually crafting one of my most powerful poems, " I Still Struggle," describing how I was coping with life after my mother's death. The open-mic nights were places where I could be honest without judgment, raw without consequences. This provided the path to writing my novels.

My victory lap should have been in 2014. A homeowner, a secure federal government job, a master's degree, a published author with two novels and a poetry book under my belt, despite every grammatical error the critics loved to point out. Instead, I stood in my living room watching contractors strip my walls down to the studs. Water damage had turned to mold, and what started as a home repair became a metaphor for my entire life. Everything looked solid on the surface, but underneath, toxicity was spreading.

The insurance covered the repairs, but they couldn't fix what was really broken. That house never felt like home again. It felt cold and dreary, like the federal office where I spent my days fighting to be seen as competent rather than angry, professional rather than just another stereotype they'd already written in their minds.

A coworker once asked if I'd been part of a "welfare-to-work program." The shock on their face when I told them yes, I was a single mother, but never on welfare. I'd started as a summer hire at seventeen and worked my way up from GS-3 to GS-12 through sheer determination and two degrees earned while raising children alone. "You're so articulate," they said, as if my intelligence was an anomaly rather than an asset. Another time, someone expressed surprise that I was from inner-city Washington, DC, as if success and that zip code were mutually exclusive.

I was drowning in a life that looked successful but felt like prison. The relationship I'd hoped would bring partnership had crumbled. The promotion I'd worked toward for years remained just out of reach, dangled like a carrot by supervisors who wanted submission, not competence. Every morning, I put on my professional mask and played a game I was destined to lose because I refused to be fake. I couldn't do it. My mouth wouldn't form the words they wanted to hear. My spine wouldn't bend the way they demanded.

The day a former coworker advised me to document everything I was doing for my resume, even if I never got the promotion, something shifted. "At least you'll be ready when something better comes along," she said. So I did. I focused on the parts of my job I could tolerate, documented every achievement, and stopped fighting for recognition from people determined not to see me. Ironically, years later, in 2017, the same supervisor who'd blocked me for years finally promoted me. They actually had to create the GS-13 position so I could apply. But by then, the damage was done. I was exhausted, bitter, and barely recognizable to myself.

Then came the Sunday that changed everything.

"If something is causing you distress," Joel Osteen said, "you have permission to walk away from it even if others call it quitting. Even if it looks like failure. Your peace is worth more than their perception."

I sat in my room and wept. Not the pretty tears of revelation, but the ugly cry of recognition. I'd been holding onto things that were killing me slowly—the house that felt like a tomb, the job that demanded I shrink myself, the American Dream that was never designed for women like me.

Within a year, I downsized from my house to an apartment. People whispered. "She's giving up." "She couldn't handle it." "What kind of example is she setting?" But for the first time in years, I could breathe. My apartment was small, but it was mine. No mold in the walls. No ghosts in the corners. Just space to think, to write, to remember who I was before I started fighting everyone else's battles.

That decision taught me something crucial: either I succeed, or I learn. There's no failure when you're moving toward your purpose. Every setback becomes data, every closed door redirects you to your actual path.

In 2019, sitting on the phone with my business coach, I said what I'd been saying for years: "I'll pursue my real dreams when I retire in 2029." I'd invested in programs with Lisa Nichols and others, but never fully engaged. Always waiting. Always planning for someday.

She listened intently but saw through my excuse. "What's it going to cost you to wait?"

I started listing the usual—time, opportunity, momentum. She stopped me.

"No, Katina. WHO is it going to cost? Who needs your voice, your story, your survival guide right now but won't get it because you're waiting for the *right* time?"

The bullet that is still lodged in my back, less than an inch from my spine, seemed to pulse. 2004. A stray bullet that should have killed me or left me paralyzed. I survived for a reason, and here I was, hoarding that survival like it was mine alone. Being selfish with the very testimony that could save someone else. How many young Black mothers were drowning in the same waters I'd learned to navigate? How many were being told their dreams had to wait until retirement, until the kids were grown, until they had permission from a world that would never grant it?

That night, I started writing the non-fiction book that had been burning in my chest for years. Not the novels I'd published despite the critics who pointed out every typo, not the poetry I'd performed on stages while working full-time, but the raw truth of what it takes to be relentless when the world expects you to disappear.

Which brings me back to that Friday afternoon in February. The early retirement offer was only available for sixty days. The financial hit would be significant. The safe choice, the smart choice, the choice everyone expected me to make was to decline. Wait four more years. Play it safe.

But I thought about my sons, now grown, who'd watched me come home defeated every night, too exhausted to write, too drained to dream. I thought about the internet radio show I'd run from 2014 to 2017, creating safe spaces for others while slowly suffocating in my own life. I thought about the manuscript sitting on my laptop, three-quarters finished, waiting for me to have the energy to complete it. I thought about the coaching clients I could serve, the stages I could speak on, the women I could lift—if only I wasn't spending all my strength surviving a job that was slowly killing my spirit.

"You're being selfish," my inner critic whispered. "Irresponsible. Reckless."

"No," I whispered back. "I'm being relentless about my purpose instead of my paycheck."

I left federal service on September 30, 2025, four years earlier than planned, thirty-three years after that nineteen-year-old girl walked into her first day of permanent employment. My last paycheck hit different. Scary different. Freedom different.

Within weeks, opportunities I couldn't have imagined started appearing. Speaking engagements. Coaching clients who needed exactly what I'd survived to teach. The energy to finish that manuscript, to show up fully for my purpose instead of dragging myself through obligation. The woman who once came home too exhausted to write now had words flowing like water.

Here's what I learned: We don't always get to choose our circumstances, but we always get to choose our responses to them. Every single day we wake up, we have the option to make changes. But we have to believe we're worthy of a better outcome. We have to stop letting others' comfort with our misery determine our choices.

I refused to let a supervisor's pettiness define my worth. I refused to let a house that was drowning me become my tomb. I refused to let "safe" become my prison. I refused to remain captive to negative thoughts that kept me stuck. Most importantly, I refused to wait until full retirement age to live my purpose when someone needed my story today.

Looking back… I am proud of my journey. I do not regret building a foundation in the federal government since my first summer job in 1990. I have my stepmother to thank for this encouragement. Some friends, family, and colleagues thought I'd lost my mind. But here's what they didn't see: I'd actually found it. For the first time in decades, I was choosing my well-being over social status, my peace over others' perceptions, my purpose over a predictable paycheck.

If you're sitting in your own version of that cubicle, that toxic house, that life that looks successful but feels like death, know this: The gap between where you are and where you want to be isn't talent or timing. It's tenacity. It's the willingness to be called crazy, irresponsible, foolish by people who are comfortable with your misery.

Some people will become content with your unhappiness and try to keep you there. They'll call your boundaries *anger*. They'll call your standards *unrealistic*. They'll call your dreams *foolish*. Let them. Their opinions are not your oxygen. Someone told me once that playing the game would be easier if I wanted to move up. But I'd rather be authentic and struggling than successful and suffocating.

You have the right to live life in your own lane, where you are the driver, not the passenger of someone else's expectations. You can create your own destination and draw your own roadmap. The American Dream doesn't have to be your dream if it's making you miserable. A temporary setback can catapult you into something better, but only if you're brave enough to let go of what's not working.

Your next decision can change everything. Don't wait for permission. Don't wait for the perfect time. Don't wait until retirement to start living your purpose. Someone needs what you've survived to learn. Someone needs your voice, your story, your relentless refusal to let circumstances write your ending.

I chose freedom over fear at fifty. I chose purpose over paycheck. I chose peace over perception. And that choice, that one terrifying, liberating, relentless choice, gave me back my life.

Be relentless about protecting your peace. Be relentless about pursuing your purpose. Be relentless about refusing to let misery win.

Your breakthrough isn't waiting for the right time. It's waiting for your next decision. Someone will love you for the same reasons others resent you. Choose the ones who celebrate your authenticity.

Be relentless.

About K.

K. Lowery Moore is an author, poet, TV show host, business owner, and empowerment speaker from Washington, DC.

In 2007, K. Lowery Moore established a publishing company, So Sophisticated Publications, to maintain sole ownership of her work. Since publishing her books, she has been featured at several literary events nationwide. She had the memorable opportunity to share her debut novel, *When I'm Loving You*, on stage at the Michael Baisden Live Tour in 2008. She also appeared on local cable TV shows in the Washington DC area: *Success Filled Living* and *Views & Vibes*.

K. Lowery Moore hosted an Internet-based TV show at Listen Vision Studios in Washington, DC. from 2014–2017. *The K. Lowery Moore Show* was formatted to discuss a myriad of topics that ignited positive conversations geared towards promoting self-love, encouraging healthy relationships, establishing businesses, reprogramming negative stereotypes, and rebuilding the family structure in the African-American community.

While raising two sons, Antonio and Andray, K. Lowery Moore earned an MBA with honors from Strayer University in 2010 and retired from federal service in 2025 after a thirty-three year career. In her spare time, she operates a networking marketing business, travels to tropical places, and spends time with family, especially her grandson, Amir.

For more information, visit Klowerymoore.com

CHAPTER 16

THE HARDEST TRYER

BY DANIEL WHITE

The trophy sat heavy in my seven-year-old hands, its weight nothing compared to the shock rippling through my chest. Six hundred kids in that Balga Little Athletics Center, and they called my name. Not for first place. Not for the fastest time. For the *hardest tryer*. The smallest kid in little athletics, perpetually last in every race, and somehow, they'd seen me. They saw the trying I didn't even know I was doing.

My legs were shaking, not from the run, but from something else… recognition. After years of being invisible, of being different in ways I couldn't name, someone had noticed I never stopped pushing. The announcer waited. "Go on, Daniel. You earned it."

Earned what, exactly? The right to be seen trying while others succeeded?

That afternoon, my parents sent me door-to-door through our neighborhood, trophy in hand. "Go and show the neighbors," my mother said. And with each knock, each surprised smile from neighbors who'd never really noticed the tiny kid on the street, something shifted. Mrs. Cocking touched the trophy as if it were pure gold. "Hardest tryer," she read aloud. "That's something special, Daniel. That's character."

Character. I rolled that word around in my mind like a marble. Was that what this burning in my chest was? This thing that made me show up to practice even when I knew I'd finish last?

I didn't know then that at this moment, this recognition of relentlessness before I even had a word for it, would become the foundation of everything I'd build. That the kid holding that trophy would one day break the four-minute mile, transform from a struggling kinesiologist to a spiritual healer working in over seventy countries, and learn to compress ten years of therapy into less than a minute of breakthrough.

But first, I had to learn what the words on this trophy really meant.

THE PATTERN OF CONSTANT CHALLENGE

A few years later, a coach approached me after watching me train. "I've been watching you," he said. "I'd like to help you. Would you like me to coach you?" His son was one of the greatest runners in the state. Everyone said yes, go for it. Under his guidance, I went from last place to third in the Center Championships for the 1,500m (the metric mile). My first medal was a notable achievement, as participation trophies were not yet a common practice. You had to earn everything.

That taste of growth became compelling. By the time I was in my teens, I'd developed a peculiar habit: whenever I started winning, I'd leave. Win at my local club? Move to a tougher one. Dominate at the state level? Move to another state where I'd come last. It wasn't arrogance. It was a desire to achieve more.

My buddy and I left our home state in 1986 and caught a train across the country to the Australian Institute of Sport Training Facility. No invitation. No connections. Just two nobody kids walking up to the coach saying, "Can we join your group?" The other athletes looked at us like we'd lost our minds. We were nobodies asking to train with the best in the country.

For the first few months, we hung onto the back of the pack, unable to talk while all the other athletes joked around and laughed. All our energy went to survival, not to be dropped by the group.

Six months later, at the national championships, those same athletes were asking what had happened. "You were nothing," one said, genuinely confused. "Now you're moving up to the top."

"I went where I was nothing, a nobody," I told him. "That's where the growth is."

This became my blueprint: find where you're last and build from there. When I started winning in Australia, I moved to the US. Back to last place. Back to building. The pattern was relentless: discomfort, struggle, growth, success, then deliberately choosing discomfort again.

Most people thought I was crazy. "Why leave when you're winning?" they'd ask. "Aren't you disappointed when you lose?" Never. Because losing meant I could improve. When I was winning too easily, other competitors would research my style to find ways to beat me. That forced me to evolve. But when winning became too comfortable, I'd get lazy. So, I'd uproot myself, find a tougher environment, and start the climb again.

The challenge itself became my fuel. Not the winning, the challenge.

BREAKING MORE THAN RECORDS

The four-minute mile had been my Everest since I was fifteen. For years, I built toward it methodically, almost boringly—one second per lap improvement. Adjust the breathing pattern. Strengthen the mental game. I treated my body like a machine, constantly upgrading it, but more importantly, I was building a foundation underneath that could hold the weight of the impossible.

The day it happened, I was alone on the track. The next runner was ten seconds behind me. No competitors pushing me. Only a small crowd cheering. Just me and the relentless rhythm of my feet against the ground. The same rhythm I'd been perfecting for years. One foot in front of the other. One breath flowing into the next. Holding onto the focus, "How fast can I run while staying relaxed?"

When I crossed the line, my coach was jumping and grabbing me. "You just broke the four!" he shouted. "No one's ever done it in this stadium!"

I hadn't even realized. I focused so much on the process, on the next step, the next breath, the next lap, that I'd blown past the barrier without noticing. That's when I learned something crucial: relentlessness isn't about the dramatic moment. It's about being so committed to the process that a breakthrough becomes inevitable.

But breaking physical barriers was just preparation for what came next.

THE SIX-YEAR WILDERNESS

By 1995, back in Australia, I had a thriving kinesiology practice, while simultaneously feeling like I was dying inside.

Something deeper was calling, past the physical work, and beyond the mental and emotional healing I was doing with clients. I knew in my heart I needed to do spiritual work. Not religious, but spiritual. Working with God's healing energy that animated everything.

The moment I made that shift, my business dropped. Clients fled. "He's lost the plot," they said. "Gone off the deep end." Friends suggested I "Get a real job." My income crashed. I was working nights at a bar to pay rent, coming home at 3 a.m. to practice energy healing techniques that no one wanted to pay for.

For six years, I pushed forward through the ridicule, debt, and well-meaning interventions from people who cared about me. Six years of others telling me I was delusional. Six years of wondering if they were right.

I remember one night, crying into my pillow, praying desperately. "God, do you want me to do this or not? Is this good for me or not?" The visions that came kept me going. One particularly dark night, the message came clear: "Put the oxygen mask on yourself first before you help others."

I realized I'd been paying everyone else—landlord, bills, everyone—with nothing left for me. That's why I was broke. Not because my path was wrong, but because I wasn't taking care of myself first. So, I changed. Pay myself first. Recover first. Build my own strength first. Then serve from fullness, not depletion.

But the lesson went deeper. I was burning out trying to give too much to too many. I had to learn to take time off, to recover, to build my own foundation. Quality became everything, but to give the best, I had to be at my best.

Then, on the seventh anniversary of my business, a great blessing was bestowed upon me. A statewide newspaper published a full-page article on my work. It generated seven months of calls. People even called me five years later, having saved the clipping "just in case." I was successful by any measure. This word-of-mouth marketing flourished for me for the next twenty years, taking me around the world working in over seventy countries.

THE QUESTION THAT CHANGED EVERYTHING

During those lean years, one client changed my entire perspective. After our session, she looked at me with tears in her eyes: "I just spent ten years in therapy on this problem, and you just got rid of it in an hour."

My first thought wasn't satisfaction. It was a question: "Why would anyone spend ten years on one problem?"

That question consumed me. If I could do it in an hour, why not ten minutes? If ten minutes, why not one? This wasn't about rushing; it was about precision. About getting so clear, so connected, so skilled that transformation happened in moments, not years.

I became relentless about compression. Every session became a laboratory. What was essential? What was just a ritual? How could I deliver the same transformation faster? I kept asking myself what I was missing. This frustration isn't failure, it's information. It's life telling you there's something you haven't learned yet.

The system I developed during those years of financial struggle became "The Financial Freedom System"—not about money itself, but about our relationship with it. About strengthening intuition so you become the boss of your circumstances, instead of their victim. The broke healer who'd been working bar shifts to pay rent wrote a book that became a three-time Amazon bestseller.

Today, I can do in under a minute what used to take an hour. I work with groups where everyone receives healing simultaneously. But my real goal? Walk into an auditorium with thousands and have everyone—100 percent, not 98 percent—receive what they need.

Because relentlessness doesn't settle for *good enough*.

THE NEVER-ENDING CHALLENGE

When my athletic career ended just before the Olympics, I thought physical challenges would be a thing of the past. I transferred all that energy into building my business, into pushing the boundaries of healing work. For decades, that was enough.

Then in 2000, I couldn't tie my shoelaces without struggling. Since retiring from athletics in 1992, I had gained half of my body weight. My body was screaming what life had been whispering: you've gotten too comfortable.

So, I started running again. One lap. Then two. Building that foundation again, just like the seven-year-old kid. Now, at almost sixty, I'm training to see how far this aging body can go. Not to compete with others, but to compete with myself. To find where I'm weak and build from there.

People ask why I put myself through it. "You're almost sixty," they say. "You've already proven yourself."

But that's not how relentlessness works. It doesn't retire. It evolves. The challenge that once lived on the running track now lives in how many people I can help simultaneously. The drive that once pushed me to break the four-minute mile now pushes me to break the barriers of what's possible in transformation work.

YOUR HARDEST TRYER MOMENT

If you're standing at your own breaking point—financial, professional, personal, or spiritual—know this: being last is not your curse. It's your curriculum.

Every rejection you've received, every time someone has underestimated you, and every moment you've felt invisible while working harder than anyone else, do not define weakness. They build your foundation and forge your relentlessness.

Remember, foundations are usually below ground, where people can't see them.

The world will tell you to find where you fit, where you're comfortable, where winning comes easily. I'm telling you the opposite: find where you're nothing and build from there. Find where trying is all you have and try harder than anyone expects.

When frustration hits, and it will, ask yourself what I always ask: "What am I missing?" Not "Why me?" but "What am I missing?" Turn frustration into curiosity. Turn obstacles into information.

Build your foundation in increments. One second per lap. One percent better each day. The dramatic breakthrough will come, but it comes disguised as ten thousand tiny victories that no one else sees.

When everyone thinks you've lost the plot, when six years feels like sixty, when you're working nights to fund your dreams, and everyone's telling you to be realistic, that's when you're closest. That's when your relentlessness matters most.

I learned to be quiet about my dreams, to work like a secret spy on my goals. Not everyone deserves to hear your vision. Find the people who support your growth, who challenge you to be better, not those who want you to stay small, so they feel comfortable.

And when no one else supports you, go straight to God and pray for guidance. The visions will come if you're willing to listen.

The gap between where you are and where you want to be isn't talent. I was the smallest, slowest kid on the track. It isn't timing. I spent six years in the wilderness while everyone thought I was crazy. It isn't connections. I walked up to that national coach as a nobody with nothing but willingness to work.

It's tenacity. It's the decision to keep trying harder than anyone expects, especially yourself. It's the willingness to see every setback as a setup for a comeback.

Your story isn't over until you say it is. Your next decision can change everything. Not your next success. Your next decision. The decision to be relentless about becoming your best self, even when challenging yourself to become that person, can sometimes be a painful process.

Be the person who moves states when winning gets too easy. Be the one who spends six years in the desert because the calling won't let you go. Be the one who starts running again at sixty because comfortable is just another word for dying.

The world needs your hardest try. It requires you to refuse to accept that your current circumstances are your final chapter. It needs you to demonstrate that persistence isn't just a nice idea. It's the only strategy that actually works.

That seven-year-old kid with the trophy didn't know he was building a life philosophy. He just knew that something inside him refused to quit. That same something is inside you.

Your trophy might not say the same as mine. It might say "breakthrough," or "finally free," or "against all odds." But underneath, it will always mean the same thing: you refused to let your current circumstances write your ending.

The world is waiting for what you'll become when you decide to be relentless. Not perfect. Not naturally gifted. Just relentless.

Your next decision can change everything.

Be relentless.

About Daniel

Daniel White is known as the world's number one spiritual coach for visionary entrepreneurs. His mission is to help them experience relentless growth and breakthroughs across all areas of their lives, creating better futures for themselves, their families, their properties, and their businesses.

For more than thirty years, he has served visionary founders, CEOs, and elite performers in more than seventy countries as an internationally recognized Energy Transformation Specialist and Executive Coach. Daniel helps his clients clear unseen energetic blockages, eliminate emotional pain, and realign with their life's mission, opening a clear path ahead.

As a best-selling author and global keynote speaker, Daniel's wisdom has been featured in international media. Through his Growth Energy Transformation System (GETS) and private engagements, Daniel supports thousands of individuals, helping them transform confusion into clarity, chaos into calm, and their pain into peace.

Grounded in the teachings of the Christ Consciousness and decades of spiritual mastery, Daniel carries a unique, God-given gift to elevate a person's body, mind, and spirit. His clients often describe his work as "ten years of struggle into one breakthrough transformation."

Scan the QR code or visit www.TheDanielWhite.com to transform your pain into peace through the Growth Energy Transformation System and achieve Relentless Growth Breakthroughs in all areas of your life.

CHAPTER 17

CHANNELING UNDERESTIMATED TO REACH REMARKABLE: HOW REFUSING TO QUIT BECAME MY SUPERPOWER

BY CRISTINA GOMEZ

The humid July morning at West Point should have broken me. Standing in formation during Cadet Basic Training, sweat drenching my uniform, I watched my classmates complete their second mile with relative ease while my lungs burned and my legs shook. I had never run two consecutive miles in my life, and here I stood at the United States Military Academy, where running was as essential as breathing. Friends had questioned my sanity. Family members had doubted my decision. Teachers had disapproved of my applying to only one school—this school.

As I sat on the floor of my barracks room, exhausted, having fallen behind on yet another run, a thought entered my mind: I just have to not quit. They'll have to kick me out for me to leave. It will not be my decision… Just don't quit.

That moment of resolve would define not just my military career but my entire approach to the seemingly impossible challenges life would have in store.

My journey to that iconic parade field began three years earlier when I visited West Point for the first time. Walking the campus, hearing the history, something inexplicable stirred within me—a pull so strong I could not imagine myself anywhere else. What Lisa Nichols might call "a fire in my belly." My guidance counselor was uneasy when she discovered I had not applied to any backup schools: "What if you don't get in?" I simply replied that I would go to the prep school and try again. Not going to West Point was not an option.

The physical requirements for admission alone nearly derailed everything. I took the fitness exam three times before finally passing. Each rejection felt like a door slamming, but I kept knocking. When the admissions officer finally said, "These scores will work—fax them immediately," I ran to the guidance office, submitted the final packet, and waited, hopeful that it would be good enough—that I would be good enough. I was the last candidate in my high school to receive an appointment to the academy. They literally pulled me out of a calculus test to deliver the news.

That first summer at West Point tested every ounce of determination I had. I focused on taking it one step at a time—left, right, left. Just get through this run, this training exercise, this task. At times, the negativity felt so potent that it left little to no room for hope of making it through the day, let alone the summer. During one particularly brutal ruck march, when whispers of doubt surrounded me, I remembered a high school classmate who had once come to my defense. He had silenced a classroom of cynics by pointing out how hard I had been working. That memory, and others like it, even if only a few, would be my fuel to keep going.

An injury would compound my fitness challenges and shadow me throughout my time at West Point. A herniated disk in my lower back became both a physical burden and a social obstacle. The injury was invisible—no cast, no crutches, nothing that signaled to others that I was fighting through genuine pain. Cadets questioned whether I was really hurt or just making excuses. That doubt stung worse than the physical pain. And I would have to work to earn back their respect with each subsequent trial.

But I had made a decision that first summer: Just don't quit—make them kick you out. I was not leaving voluntarily. So I modified my training, learned to strengthen different muscle groups, and kept pushing forward. Over the next four years, I would try and fail what felt like a million times, in almost every physical feat. I had to grab hold of each victory, no matter how small, and build a foundation of strength for the next challenge, which would always come. Six months after graduation, I completed something that would have seemed laughable to that struggling new cadet: a marathon. The girl who couldn't run two miles crossed a finish line after 26.2 miles.

My time at West Point not only defined how I would personally approach tough challenges but also how I would face them when leading a team. During my senior year, I decided to bring the American Cancer Society's Relay for Life to campus. We hit a huge roadblock almost immediately—military installations have restrictions against hosting such events on government property. Instead of accepting that, I walked straight into my law professor's office and asked: "How do we make this possible?" Together, we found a way.

That first Cadet Relay for Life took place at the local junior high just off base and raised more than $80,000. I had built the team, designed the plan, and led its execution, accounting for every single detail, every mini-step needed to achieve something initially thought to be too difficult.

Even before we had become platoon leaders, it was incredible to see what a clear vision and a dedicated group could accomplish. It was truly remarkable.

Being underestimated and proving others wrong became a recurring theme, but with each successful assignment, not only did I build confidence, I also gained a small distinct group of supporters—advisors who believed in me, understood what I was capable of, and helped me take opportunities to showcase that. I was put in roles of increasing responsibility, well above my rank. The bar kept getting higher and higher, making the pool of doubters larger and larger. But I had my people, the ones who recognized the depths of my potential, even when I didn't.

As if by serendipity, this path led me back to where it all began, working on the West Point Staff, tasked with establishing a whole new team and providing a whole new capability. Despite the support of key leaders, there was still a palpable skepticism when I arrived.

I dove into the job with the same determination that had carried me through West Point the first time. I studied the mission requirements, built relationships across departments, and approached each project as a chance to exceed expectations. After my first briefing to the superintendent, it all seemed to click. I had succeeded in gaining clear guidance, decisions, and approval. After that meeting, fellow staff members were more eager to collaborate—I had proven myself yet again.

During this second stint at West Point, ten years into my career, I felt a familiar restlessness—a fire in my belly for something new, something more. I even considered leaving the Army altogether, but my old platoon sergeant implored me to "stay in and just keep going." He knew what I could do, having seen it firsthand in Afghanistan. So, when a mentor and friend introduced me to the Army's strategist branch—a highly competitive track involving strategic planning and complex problem-solving—it seemed like just the right fit. There were two ways to become a strategist: apply for an Army-internal, specialty transfer or apply through the Harvard Kennedy School. One thing was certain: I was going to be a strategist. It was just a question of whether or not I was going to be a Harvard strategist.

This time, the doubts were all mine. Me, a product of the Alabama public school system, with a less-than-extraordinary undergrad transcript, go to Harvard? But my boss saw something I was still learning to recognize in myself. "Don't self-select out," he urged. For the Harvard Strategist Program, I would have to get through two major hurdles: first, getting Army approval to attend, and second, gaining acceptance to the school itself.

A little over a year later, I was standing in Harvard Yard. The moment felt surreal, but also familiar. It was the same feeling I had had when I stepped into my first classroom at West Point. "I made it." These moments had become about even more than proving others wrong. They were about continuing to prove to myself that refusing to quit creates possibilities beyond imagination. They were about reaching for remarkable.

The word *remarkable* entered my world when the same professor who had helped me with Relay For Life, years later, told me something I will never forget. "You have a passion for being remarkable." I was speechless. I was flattered, sure, but I was still struggling to own my strengths and overcome my insecurities. I had no idea how to respond. He continued, providing evidence for his assessment: You wanted to join the Army—you went to West Point. You wanted to overcome your physical struggles—you did a marathon. You wanted to go to grad school and become a strategist—you went to Harvard.

All of these choices throughout my life laid out a pattern that even I had not noticed. Somewhere along the way, consciously or unconsciously, I had decided to shoot for the moon and not settle for a star. Whether I was battling my circumstances or myself, I was channeling that feeling of being underestimated into being remarkable.

This philosophy now shapes and drives so much of my life, including my latest venture, the latest fire in my belly: "Consulting Remarcable." I am building a firm that is dedicated to helping its clients define and achieve their goals—define and achieve their *remarcable*. Remarcable, with a *c* instead of *k*, to reinforce the importance of writing our own unique story and to highlight how the firm tailors its services to each unique client.

With this company, I hope to share what I have learned about turning obstacles into opportunities, about fighting for what you want, and about refusing to quit when quitting would be perfectly logical.

Recently, at my promotion ceremony, just after pinning Lieutenant Colonel, my uncle pulled me aside with an admission that punctuated my journey to this point. "We didn't think you'd make it through West Point," he said, "let alone sixteen years in the Army." His honesty didn't sting—it validated every moment I had chosen to persist when stopping would have been easier.

Applying to West Point taught me a crucial lesson about self-advocacy. When I kept hearing "no" from what seemed like every direction, I realized that the strongest advocacy can reveal not just what we want, but what we are willing to fight for. That act of fighting for something and refusing to accept closed doors uncovers what truly matters to us. I knew that I had to be a part of the Long Gray Line. What I didn't know was that it would be the origin story for all the future obstacles I would overcome.

My commitment to vision has always required three elements I discovered along the way. First, there must be a strong "why," a strong purpose to fuel the fight, even if it is an inexplicable emotional pull like what I felt at West Point. Second, confidence builds through intermediate successes, even if seemingly infinitesimal. Each improved run time, each successful project, each "yes" after multiple "no's" becomes a building block for the next challenge. Third, maintain a strong board of advisors. Lean on those few key individuals who understand your drive, support your success, and drown out the doubt.

There is one quote that has gotten me through the roughest moments, though very few people know it has been my anchor. It comes from a poem by Marianne Williamson, though I first heard it in the movie *Coach Carter*: "Our deepest fear is not that we are inadequate. Our deepest fear is that we are powerful beyond measure. It is our light, not our darkness, that most frightens us." The full poem speaks to how our brightness gives others permission to shine.

This truth explains why being remarkable is not about ego, but instead about showing others what is possible when we refuse to let circumstances write our story. It is our responsibility to be as remarkable as we can, and that in and of itself can scare us into doubt, scare us into settling. Instead, we must shine.

Looking back at that struggling new cadet who couldn't run two miles, I see someone who didn't yet understand her own power. But she had one crucial quality: she refused to quit. That refusal became a practice, then a habit, then a superpower. It pushed me through a marathon, through deployments, through Harvard, through demanding positions designed for officers senior to me.

Here's what I know after over sixteen years of military service, having stood on the precipice of a breakthrough moment: self-awareness is crucial. The kind that helps you recognize what excites you, what terrifies you in the best way, what makes you lean forward instead of shrinking back. The kind that helps you understand your self-doubt to then overcome it. When you feel that pull toward something that seems impossible, pay attention. Ask yourself how you would feel if that opportunity suddenly disappeared. If the thought makes you sick, that's your answer.

The problems in front of you will always seem overwhelming if you stare at the entire mountain. But every mountain is climbed one step at a time—left, right, left. Focus on the immediate challenge, then the next one, then the one after that. Before you know it, you will be standing at a summit you once thought unreachable, ready to spot the next peak on the horizon.

Being relentless is not about being superhuman. It is about being unwilling to let our current circumstances determine our final story. It's about recognizing that every "no" contains information about the next approach, that every setback is data for our comeback, that every person who underestimates us is giving us an opportunity to expand their imagination and our own, to help them shine as we do.

If you are standing at your own West Point moment—facing something that terrifies you, something others say you cannot do, something that highlights more weaknesses than strengths—know this: the gap between where you are and where you want to be is not talent or timing. It's tenacity. Your next decision can change everything.

Be remarkable. Be relentless.

About Cristina

Cristina Gomez has served in the U.S. Army for over fifteen years, excelling in the fields of planning and operations, strategy and policy, stakeholder engagement, and leadership. Known for her professional acumen and tenacious work ethic, Cristina has led multidisciplinary teams in providing commanders, partners, and decision-makers with creative solutions for a wide range of challenges.

Cristina is an Army Strategist, a Lieutenant Colonel on active duty, currently stationed at U.S. Southern Command in Doral, Florida. Since commissioning from the U.S. Military Academy at West Point, she has served in various organizations, including tactical units in Afghanistan and Kuwait, operational commands in Germany and Turkey, and strategic headquarters at the Pentagon. A recipient of the Harvard Kennedy School Lucius N. Littauer Fellows Award, Cristina has consistently demonstrated excellence, community-building, and effective leadership with each new professional endeavor. Cristina is also the Founder of *Consulting Remarcable*, a firm dedicated to helping its clients to define and achieve their goals—to define and achieve their "remarcable."

Whether it's a platoon or a company, a staff or a board, a class or a team, Cristina has a passion for leading diverse groups to solve complex problems. Cristina is trusted by her peers and supervisors alike to not only get the job done, but to get it done remarkably well.

Outside of work, Cristina enjoys cooking, dancing, traveling, and spending time with her friends and family—especially her 120-pound Alaskan Malamute, Optimus Prime.

CHAPTER 18

THE DAY I REFUSED TO BE A STATISTIC

BY JAMES "JW" RADFORD

The neurologist's words hung in the sterile air like a death sentence: "Multiple sclerosis. Incurable. You'll probably end up in a wheelchair. Likely blind. Here's your medication. You will inject it into your thigh muscle once a week. You'll feel like you have the flu for three to four days afterward. Good luck."

I sat there in my military uniform, the same uniform I'd worn with pride for years, planning to make the service my career until retirement. Twenty minutes earlier, I'd walked into that office thinking I'd just damaged a nerve lifting weights. Now, well-meaning doctors erased my entire future, military career, health, and independence with clinical efficiency. They delivered devastation as if they were reading a weather report.

The following weeks blurred into a haze of depression. The military quickly determined I was no longer qualified for my position. Career gone. Health deteriorating. Marriage crumbling under the weight of a diagnosis neither of us had signed up for. I found myself a single father of four daughters, trying to hold together a life that was systematically falling apart.

For two years, I lived in denial. I stopped taking the medication. I couldn't face jamming that needle into my thigh week after week. I knew it would make me sick for days. I knew it only managed symptoms of something that would eventually win anyway. I lied to my doctors during checkups, pretended everything was fine, and waited for the inevitable.

THE MOMENT EVERYTHING CHANGED

The moment that changed everything wasn't dramatic. No lightning bolts or heavenly choirs. Just me, standing at an ATM outside a Chipotle, four hungry daughters waiting in the car, and a bank account so empty I couldn't even withdraw money for their dinner.

I stood there, staring at that "Insufficient Funds" message, and something inside me snapped, or maybe something inside me finally woke up. In Korean culture, they call it *satori*, which translates to sudden enlightenment. For me, it was simpler: This can't be it.

I looked back at my daughters in the car, trusting me to provide something as basic as dinner, and made a decision that would define the next sixteen years of my life. I didn't care if I ended up in a wheelchair. I didn't care if I went blind. My daughters were going to have their Chipotle, and more importantly, they were going to have a father who refused to surrender to statistics.

That night, I made a promise to myself: I was going after everything I'd ever dreamed of. MS might be incurable, but giving up was a choice, and I refused to make it.

BUILDING FROM NOTHING

Starting Trust Consulting Services as a government contracting company while battling MS and raising four daughters alone required relentlessness born from having nothing left to lose.

I knew nothing about government contracting. Access to capital? None. Understanding of how to write winning proposals? Zero. Knowledge of managing employees and meeting payroll? Laughable. But I had something more valuable than expertise: I had already been handed my worst-case scenario by those doctors, and I was still standing.

The first months were brutal. I submitted proposal after proposal, each rejection adding weight to the voice in my head whispering that the doctors were right. I should accept my limitations, scale down my dreams, and prepare for the wheelchair.

Instead, I got angry. Then I got smart.

I realized my problem wasn't the disease, the market, or the economy. My problem was isolation. Success in government contracting, like success in any field, happens in community. So, I started showing up to networking events, business conferences, and anywhere successful contractors gathered. I couldn't afford most of these events, but I went anyway, sometimes volunteering just to get in the door.

At one conference, an older contractor pulled me aside. "You're going about this all wrong," he said. "Nobody gets their first contract alone. Partner with someone established. Sub-contract under them. Learn the business while you earn."

That advice changed everything. Within months, I had my first subcontract. Years later, I would take over that same contract as the prime contractor. But first, I had to prove I belonged in rooms where nobody expected to see someone like me.

THE HALF-MILLION DOLLAR GAMBLE

My first prime contract, a solo contract the government awarded directly to me, arrived with impossible requirements. It was a security contract that required metal detectors, screening equipment, and security protocols I'd never handled before. The equipment alone would cost half a million dollars. I had maybe five hundred in my business account.

I Googled frantically, finally finding a supplier in Italy.

The phone call that followed required every ounce of audacity I'd developed since my diagnosis. I convinced an Italian equipment supplier to ship me half a million dollars' worth of security equipment with no money down, no credit history, and no collateral. All I had to offer was my word and the passion in my voice that must have transcended the language barrier.

When the equipment arrived at the government facility before I expected it, the contracting officer called. "James, do you have some walk-through metal detectors coming?"

"Of course," I said, my heart pounding. "Of course I do."

Then came the next impossibility: hire sixty-four security guards in two weeks. I borrowed a conference room, posted ads everywhere, and interviewed twenty candidates at a time. People thought I was crazy. Maybe I was. But that contract, awarded in 2016, is still mine today.

THREE HUNDRED GUARDS IN A PANDEMIC

If that first security contract tested my resourcefulness, COVID-19 demanded something beyond relentlessness. It required operating on pure faith.

The call came as Maryland's hospitals overflowed with patients. The state was converting the Baltimore Convention Center into a temporary hospital. They needed security. Three hundred guards. Pricing by tomorrow. Start date: immediately.

I had never managed anything close to three hundred security personnel. But when medical professionals have already told you you'll end up blind and paralyzed, when you've already rebuilt from nothing once, *impossible* becomes just another word for *figure it out*.

I worked through the night calculating pricing. When I won the contract, reality hit: I needed to hire, uniform, and deploy three hundred security guards in Baltimore in the middle of a pandemic when nobody wanted to leave their homes.

I posted on every platform imaginable. Nearly a thousand people showed up that first weekend. The line wrapped around the building. Baltimore police had to manage the crowd. Some applicants showed up intoxicated. They just needed work that badly. I understood that desperation.

I drove to Baltimore in the middle of the night, finding my guards lost, trying to locate their posts. I'd see someone in one of our uniforms wandering the streets and pull over: "You looking for your post? Jump in."

The equipment, uniforms, and logistics—every element required me to become someone I didn't know I could be. But failure wasn't an option. When opportunity arrives at this scale, walking through the door isn't courage; it's necessity.

SIXTEEN YEARS OF DEFYING PREDICTIONS

Throughout all of this, MS lurked in the background, the timer the doctors had set ticking steadily. After two years of denying my diagnosis and skipping medication, my body finally rebelled. I was walking one day when my leg simply stopped working. Just stopped, like someone had cut the power.

The doctors' reaction was predictable: aggressive medication, prepare for the wheelchair within a year, and start making arrangements. That was sixteen years ago.

Today, I run in Spartan races. I rock climb. I snorkel and rappel down waterfalls. I'm in the best shape of my life, defying every projection those doctors made. My neurologist shakes his head at every monthly appointment, baffled by my continued mobility and health.

But it's not a medical miracle, it's a mindset. When that exacerbation hit, and my leg failed, it shook me. But it also woke me up again. If I needed medication, I'd take medication. If I needed rehab, I'd do rehab. Whatever it took, I would do it, because I had finally understood a fundamental truth: I was writing my own story, and this wasn't the ending.

THE POWER OF RELENTLESS PASSION

People often ask how I convinced banks to lend money to someone with no financial history, how I persuaded suppliers to ship equipment without payment, and how I secured government contracts despite having no experience. The answer isn't strategy. It's passion that burns so hot it ignites everyone it touches.

When my first ten-million-dollar contract came through, traditional banks laughed. "Come back in three years when you have financials," they said. "Maybe we'll loan you a hundred thousand then." But I had employees to pay now, not in three years.

I turned to alternative financing, which was asset-based lending, where lenders looked at contracts instead of credit history. Even they required convincing. But when you're driven by something deeper than logic, when your very survival depends on success, you don't speak words, you transmit energy. Those lenders didn't just hear a business proposition. They heard someone whose relentlessness made him a safer bet than any spreadsheet. They fronted me payroll money before the paperwork was even complete.

This passion—this rocket fuel born from refusing to accept your prescribed ending—doesn't just change you. It changes everyone around you. Your risk-averse attorney wife starts believing. Strangers become allies. Impossibilities become inconveniences.

DESTINY CALLS THROUGH ADVERSITY

Here's what I need you to understand if you're standing at your own breaking point, staring at your own version of that ATM screen or that doctor's diagnosis: Destiny always calls through trouble.

If I had never been diagnosed with MS, I wouldn't be here today. That diagnosis wasn't my ending; it was my beginning. Every progression in life, from one stage to another, is preceded by what feels like destruction. The child must die for the adolescent to be born. The employee must fail for the entrepreneur to emerge.

We run from these moments. We see the cliff edge and scramble backward. But it's not a cliff, it's a doorway. And the only way through is to lean into the thing that terrifies you most.

When I accepted my diagnosis—really accepted it, not as a limitation but as my call to greatness—everything changed. I decided that if I were going to end up in a wheelchair, it would be after I'd run every race I wanted to run. If I were going blind, it would be after I'd seen everything I wanted to see. And maybe, just maybe, if I lived with enough relentlessness, those prophecies would never come true at all.

YOUR NEXT DECISION DEFINES YOU

Sixteen years later, I'm still here. Still standing. Still building. Still refusing to be a statistic. Not because I'm special, but because I learned the secret that changes everything: setbacks don't define you, your next decision does.

Somewhere inside you lives the child who believed anything was possible, who saw the world as infinite, who knew you could be anything you imagined. That child didn't die. They just got buried under diagnoses and divorces, failures and fears, bank balances and bad news.

But that passionate, creative, unstoppable force is still there, waiting for you to make the decision I made standing at that ATM: This can't be it.

Your version of MS might be bankruptcy, divorce, job loss, or dreams deferred so long you've forgotten what hoping feels like. The specifics don't matter. What matters is your next decision. Will you accept the statistics, the projections, the *realistic* assessments of your limitations? Or will you become relentless?

The world needs your story of transformation. Your struggle isn't just yours. It's the proof someone else needs that their situation isn't permanent. Your breakthrough becomes someone else's possibility.

So, lean into the difficulty. Sprint toward the thing that scares you. Refuse to let anything, not disease, poverty, or a world that underestimates you, write your ending. You're not too late, but it will take relentlessness.

Once you decide to be relentless, once you refuse to accept *this is it*, once you start moving with the passion of someone who has nothing to lose and everything to gain, doors open. Resources appear. The impossible becomes inevitable.

Your story isn't over. It's just beginning. Be relentless.

About JW

James "JW" Radford is a U.S. Air Force veteran, former federal Contracting Officer, and the visionary founder and CEO of Trust Consulting Services, a powerhouse government contracting firm with over $70 million in annual revenue and more than 1,700 employees nationwide. As a nationally recognized best-selling author and inspirational speaker, Radford shares his journey of resilience and leadership to uplift veterans, entrepreneurs, and underserved communities. He is also the founder of the Courage to Climb Foundation, which empowers individuals overcoming adversity. Outside of work, JW is a devoted family man who finds joy in mentoring youth, exploring new business ventures, and indulging in his passion for good food, sports, and spontaneous weekend adventures. Whether he's leading from the boardroom or motivating from the stage, JW Radford brings energy, purpose, and a deep commitment to impact wherever he goes.

CHAPTER 19

THE FORGOTTEN TV TAPES: HOW THE EXILE IN THE ARCHIVE BECAME THE PATH TO AN UNEXPECTED CAREER

BY TERRY INGLESE

The fluorescent lights of the Swiss Public Television archives hummed above me as I held another box of TV videotapes—someone else's work, someone else's success story. Six months earlier, I'd been producing one of the network's most successful animation programs. Three years of weekly episodes, fifty-two weeks a year, reaching viewers across Switzerland and northern Italy. Now, I was filing those memories away, literally archiving the creative output of colleagues who still had their TV shows while mine had been cancelled in a single budget meeting.

Year 2003; the words of the Swiss Public Television director still echo. "We're cutting your program." No discussion. No transition plan. Just an abrupt end to everything I'd built, followed by what felt like professional exile to the basement archives. From a respected young TV producer to a filing clerk in one devastating conversation. Everyone would have understood if I'd quit that day. The humiliation was complete. My colleagues avoided eye contact in the hallways. Some offered pitying smiles. Others pretended not to see me at all.

But I refused to let that basement become my grave.

THE BACKSTORY: WHEN SUCCESS MEANT NOTHING

Three years earlier, I'd pitched what seemed impossible: a program that would appeal to everyone, not just children. The executives had been skeptical about a weekly TV show about animation for everyone. In Switzerland? The conservative broadcasting culture suggested I was proposing career suicide. But I'd done my research, prepared meticulously, read and studied cinema literature, considered international markets, interviewed animation film directors, followed the animation trends by enthusiastically participating in film festivals all over Europe, like the Festival international du film d'animation of Annecy in France, the Stuttgart International Festival of Animated Film in Germany and the Fantoche Internationales Festival für Animationsfilm of Baden in Switzerland … and most importantly, I believed in the vision with every fiber of my being.

My TV show, called "Animanotte," or *The Night Soul of Animation*, exceeded all expectations. Week after week, for three consecutive years, we presented "short movies never seen before" that challenged perceptions about what animation could be. We weren't just showing cartoons. We were exploring animation, showcasing the work of international creators and artists, presenting and explaining diverse animation techniques, interviewing animation pioneers, and discovering young talents. Critics praised our innovative approach. TV viewers wrote letters, actual handwritten letters in the early 2000s, thanking us for bringing something completely "fresh" to the Swiss Public Television panorama. Parents watched with their children. Cinema scholars and film students applauded us for our work. Artists tuned in for inspiration, and for a couple of years, I was president of the Swiss Animation Group, representing many Swiss artists at international film festivals. I was happy and enthusiastic. I'd found my calling, or so I thought.

What I didn't understand back then was that success in large organizations isn't just about results. It's about politics, budgets, and invisible battles fought in boardrooms where creators aren't invited. When new management arrived with different priorities and tighter budgets, my innovative TV program became expendable. Three years of consistent ratings, critical acclaim, and audience loyalty meant nothing when balanced against a spreadsheet. The decision wasn't personal, they assured me. It was just business.

The demotion to the TV archives wasn't just a professional punishment; it was likely meant to make me quit. They couldn't fire me outright under Swiss employment law, but they could make my daily existence so humiliating that I'd leave voluntarily. "Place the ambitious young producer among dusty TV archived tapes and forgotten programs. Let her file away other people's achievements while her own withered in those windowless rooms."

THE JOURNEY THROUGH: GOLD HIDDEN IN A SPECIAL BOX OF FORGOTTEN TV TAPES

For weeks, while working in the archives, my frustration boiled and felt like acid in my veins. I'd built something meaningful, created a TV show that mattered, and now I was archiving other people's work from inventory logs, updating database entries, and organizing shelves of obsolete formats. A colleague producer's words rang in my head: "Look to what's next." Easy for him to say; he still had his own TV show running. The irony wasn't lost on me.

But something stubborn inside me refused to surrender. Maybe it was my Italian heritage, that passionate refusal to accept defeat. Maybe it was my Swiss sense of discipline, the methodical commitment to see things through. Whatever it was, I kept showing up. Day after day, box after box, videotape after videotape, and I refused to give them the satisfaction of my resignation.

Then came the box that changed everything.

A colleague from the educational department casually asked me to archive "some old interviews". That box had been sitting, ignored, in a corner for years, gathering dust. When I watched the first videotape, I expected another forgettable series destined for permanent storage. Instead, I discovered a real treasure: hours of TV interviews conducted in the 70s, 80s, and 90s with world-renowned thinkers and scholars—philosophers, educators, scientists, artists—whose work I'd only known through dense academic texts. Here was Umberto Eco discussing semiotics with the passion of a storyteller. There was Noam Chomsky on linguistics, making complex theories accessible. I found interviews with philosophers like Michel Foucault, Karl Popper, and Paul Feyerabend, the anthropologist Claude Lévi-Strauss, the psychologists Carl Jung and Jean Piaget, and others sharing their insightful and pivotal scholarly paradigms. Tape after tape revealed more gold, all captured in their prime, explaining their life's work.

These weren't just interviews! They were hidden masterclasses slowly degrading in an archive basement, while students struggled through impenetrable academic texts, never knowing these scholars and thinkers had been captured on film, made accessible, made human.

My hands shook as I catalogued each of them. The irony was almost too perfect. Here I was, punished for making animation accessible to everyone, discovering academic content that desperately needed to be made accessible to students and to educators. A vibrant idea began forming, wild and audacious. What if I could bring these videotapes directly into the university classrooms? What if I could study how students would learn— differently—when they could see and hear these scholars instead of just reading their words in written texts? What if the very medium that had betrayed me, the television, could become a new ally and the vehicle for an academic revolution in multimedia learning?

The plan was insane: leave my stable job at the television, enroll in a PhD program, even without much academic background beyond my basic degree, and finally transform myself from a TV producer into a multimedia educational researcher. Use my disgrace as a launching pad for something entirely different. I had no research experience, no academic publications, and no scholarly network, yet! All I had was a box of TV videotapes, a contract allowing me to use these interviews for educational purposes, and a burning desire to prove that my intuition and my skills were precious and worthy.

THE TURNING POINT: WHEN REJECTION BECAME ROCKET FUEL

I quit the Swiss Public Television on a Thursday afternoon. My supervisor seemed relieved—one less reminder of management's poor decisions walking the hallways. By Monday, I was at the University, proposing a PhD focused on the educational use of TV archives transformed into multimedia learning content. My research question was born of those basement archives: How would students engage with and learn from academic content when it is presented through audiovisual media (*the audiovisual authors*) versus traditional text (*the invisible authors*)?

The academic world initially viewed me with suspicion. Who was this young TV producer thinking she could contribute to educational research? The rejection was familiar, almost comforting. But I'd learned something in that archive basement: rejection is just redirection, if you're relentless enough. I had something my academic peers didn't: years of practical experience in creating engaging TV shows and multimedia content. I understood not just the theory but the craft of visual storytelling, the rhythm of engagement, the architecture of attention, and the awe for beauty.

The real breakthrough came when Professor Richard E. Mayer at the University of California, Santa Barbara, agreed to supervise part of my research. Mayer is a legend in multimedia learning and in the so-called *science of instruction*, and somehow, my unconventional background intrigued him. I was heading to California to study with one of the world's leading experts in cognitive psychology and multimedia learning. These TV videotapes, meant to be forgotten, became the foundation for innovative research into how visual and auditory channels affect comprehension, retention, and learning with purpose and interest.

California transformed everything. At UCSB, my television background wasn't a liability; it was an asset. I could discuss multimedia experiments that actually engaged students because I understood engagement from a practitioner's perspective. My dissertation didn't just earn me a PhD; it opened doors I never knew existed. Universities invited me to lecture. Conferences requested presentations. Later, the School of Business of a Swiss University of Applied Sciences and Arts offered me a teaching position. The very skills that the Swiss Public Television had deemed worthless, like storytelling, multimedia communication, and making complex ideas accessible, became my real assets.

THE TRANSFORMATION FRAMEWORK: FROM THE TV ARCHIVE TO BREAKTHROUGH INTO HIGHER EDUCATION

The journey from that archive to academic success taught me principles I now teach my students:

1. **Your defeats are data, not destiny.** That archive room wasn't my ending. It was research for my next chapter. Every setback contains

information about what to do differently, where to pivot, and how to evolve. When I teach data visualization, academic writing, and critical thinking now, I tell students that the most interesting insights often come from failure points, from anomalies, from what doesn't fit the pattern.

2. **Revenge projects fuel relentless action.** When they cancelled my TV show, I started my own documentary. When they said I couldn't be creative, I found creativity in academia. When they tried to make me invisible, I became impossible to ignore. Channel your anger and frustration into ambitious actions. Let them watch you build something they never imagined from the wreckage they created.

3. **The box that seems like punishment might hold your purpose.** Those TV videotapes were meant to bury me in obscurity. Instead, they became my bridge to a new career. Sometimes what looks like exile is actually a preparation for an expedition. The very thing designed to diminish you might be the raw material for your elevation and for the unfolding of your new professional self.

4. **Break the impossible *big* into small, feasible *parts*.** "*Challenging but feasible*" became my mantra for life reconstruction. A PhD first, followed by a documentary, and an MBA later seemed impossible until I broke it into semesters, courses, chapters, paragraphs, sentences, and words. Every mountain is just a series of steps. Every transformation is just one decision followed by another.

5. **Your unique background is your competitive advantage.** Academia didn't need another traditional researcher. It needed someone who understood how to make a scholarship engaging. Your unconventional path isn't a liability—it's your differentiator. Those years in television weren't wasted; they were the preparation for a contribution only I could make.

6. **Build your network from the ashes of your bridges.** When I left television, I thought I was burning bridges. Instead, I was creating space for new connections. Jack Canfield's principles, which I'd studied for years, suddenly made sense: success isn't just about what you know or even who you know—it's about whom you become through your struggles.

THE CALL FORWARD: YOUR ARCHIVE AWAITS

If you're reading this from your own archive, literal or metaphorical, know this: the insurmountable obstacle trying to bury you might be planting you for extraordinary growth. That job that ended, that opportunity that vanished, that door that slammed shut—these aren't conclusions. They're invitations to become relentless about your own transformation.

Success isn't about avoiding archive moments; it's about what you do when you're down there. It's about refusing to accept that someone else's decision about your value is the final verdict. It's about understanding that "*challenging but feasible*" applies to your entire life, not just your projects.

Today, I teach storytelling and data visualization, academic writing, and critical thinking to business students and do research on AI literacy. I show them how to make complex information accessible, engaging, and memorable. But what I'm really teaching them is what those basement archives taught me: Your current circumstances are just raw material. Your setbacks are a setup for something better. Your willingness to keep showing up when everything says quit—that's where transformation lives.

My documentary about Giordano Bruno, the Renaissance philosopher burned at the stake of the Inquisition for defending his ideas in 1600? I finished it. The one that the Swiss Public Television in Lugano also had rejected multiple times. Three years of my own money, countless days and nights of work, equipment borrowed ... an endeavor that reminded me that every rejection from the TV became fuel. Every "no" pushed me harder. The young TV producer they'd tried to bury became a documentary filmmaker, an educational researcher in multimedia learning and media literacy, and now she is a university lecturer. Because when you've been professionally burned alive, you understand something about resurrection. You understand that giving up is the only real death. Giordano Bruno refused to recant his beliefs even as the flames rose. I refused to recant my creative vision even as my career turned to ash.

The Spanish Camino de Santiago, which I walked alone during my darkest period, taught me something essential: Every journey is just one step, then another, then another. "*Step by step*" is another powerful mantra of mine. You don't have to see the destination. You just have to keep moving. The pilgrims you are meeting along the way, sharing their own stories of why they walk—they remind you that everyone is fighting their own battle, walking away from something, walking toward something else.

That archive you're sitting in right now? Those videotapes you're being forced to file? They're not your prison. They're your portal. The gap between where you are and where you want to be isn't timing—it's tenacity. That dead-end job, that failed project, that rejection letter—these are not verdicts. They're raw material for your comeback story.

Look closer at what's in that box they've handed you. Your breakthrough might be labeled as someone else's debris. Your next chapter might be hiding in what everyone else has forgotten. Sometimes the universe's greatest gifts come wrapped in rejection letters, delivered to basement archives, hidden in boxes nobody else wants to open.

Never give up. Especially when giving up would make perfect sense. That's when being relentless matters the most. Your story isn't over. It's being archived for the comeback documentary you're about to direct.

Be relentless. Your resurrection is waiting.

About Terry

Terry Inglese (PhD, MBA) works at the School of Business at a University of Applied Sciences and Arts in Switzerland, where she serves as a lecturer in Business Communication, Academic Writing, Storytelling in Data Visualization, and Critical Thinking. Her research focuses on the psychology of learning, instructional design, didactics with new technologies, and, more recently, artificial intelligence literacy.

Before entering academia, Terry spent nearly a decade between one of the three Swiss Public Television stations and a regional TV station in Switzerland, where she designed cultural TV programs, produced documentaries, directed her own documentary, and coordinated workflows among journalists and technical teams. During this time, she also developed and tested an educational model using TV multimedia archives—work that later evolved into her PhD research in multimedia learning in higher education.

Following her doctoral studies, Terry served for about 5 years as a postdoctoral researcher and lecturer at the University of California, Santa Barbara (UCSB), where she continued experimenting and exploring innovative approaches to learning with multimedia and multimodality.

In her free time, she enjoys sharing her passion for teaching Italian language and culture.

CHAPTER 20

THE COST OF NOT TRYING

BY ANGEL J. SPEAR

"You only made six hundred dollars this month. You need to find something else to do."

My ex-husband's words landed sharp, shattering, and final, like a punch straight to my gut. I stood there in our beautiful Georgia apartment, my clothes still reeking of Hair Spritz and the smoke of hot curlers from the salon, my five-year-old son Gabriel playing with his trucks in the living room. Thirty days. I'd been a professional hairstylist for exactly thirty days, and here was the man who'd promised to love and support me, telling me to quit.

On paper, he was right. Six hundred dollars wouldn't cover rent in Georgia. It barely covered groceries. Any reasonable person would have seen the logic in his assessment. But something inside me ignited into pure determination. Maybe it was the same fire that had kept me in school when everyone else was dropping out. This was the same stubborn refusal that made me keep my baby at seventeen when abortion seemed like the only *smart* choice.

"Watch me," I said. Not to him, but to myself, the universe, and to every statistic that said a Black teen mom from the inner city would never amount to anything.

That moment taught me the most expensive lesson of my life: You can't measure the cost of not trying in dollars lost. It's measured in dreams deferred, in generations stuck in the same cycles, in the quiet death of possibility that happens when we let other people's limitations become our own.

THE PRICE OF STAYING SMALL

Growing up in inner-city New York, I learned early that there were two currencies: survival and escape. Most people around me were spending everything they had on survival. They bought drugs to numb the pain, alcohol to forget the limitations, and quick hustles to make it through another day. I watched my mother choose her addiction over her children, leaving me essentially to raise myself from age twelve. I watched friends drop out of school, lose their lives, get arrested, and get lost in the system designed to keep us exactly where we were.

But my father, despite his own struggles, gave me glimpses of escape. He'd take me to open houses in neighborhoods we'd never afford, flip through fashion magazines showing me worlds beyond our block. "Look at this, Angel," he'd say, pointing to some glossy spread of a penthouse apartment. "This exists. People live like this." He wasn't promising me that life. He was showing me it was possible.

Those glimpses became my inspiration. Not money, not connections, but the radical idea that there was something beyond what I could see from my front porch.

When I got pregnant at seventeen, everyone had opinions about my future. Teachers shook their heads. Family members offered condolences as if I'd died. Some asked questions like, "Are you sure about keeping it?" and "What are you going to do with a baby?" Friends who were teen moms themselves welcomed me to the club of limited possibilities. The message was unanimous: Your life is over before it started. That began to feel true. My home life became increasingly heavy as my mother's addiction and denial grew. My spirit knew that to give my baby a chance, I needed a reset. So, in August of 1997, I packed up what little belongings I had, took a deep breath, and crossed the country to Corpus Christi, Texas, to live with my brother Tony.

October 14, 1997, while holding Gabriel for the first time, feeling his tiny fingers wrap around mine, I made a decision that would cost me everything and give me everything in return. I wouldn't just survive, I would thrive. Not in spite of him, but because of him. This child didn't ask to be born to a seventeen-year-old girl with no money and limited prospects. In that moment, I decided I would do whatever it took because he deserved better than what statistics promised him. We both did.

THE CURRENCY OF DETERMINATION

School became my sanctuary. While other teen moms were dropping out, I showed up every day. I was blessed to have my brother Tony. Although he was only five years older, he was determined to guide me as much as he could. He kept me motivated, encouraged me, and watched Gabriel every day while I went to class. After school, I would do homework while he napped and studied for tests while breastfeeding. Hair became my freedom. Starting at eleven years old, I'd charge fifteen dollars to style hair, learning that my hands could create both beauty and income.

People ask me how I did it, and the truth is simpler than they expect: I couldn't afford not to. Every moment I wanted to quit, every time the exhaustion felt unbearable, I'd look at Gabriel and calculate the cost. The cost of giving up wasn't just my dreams; it was his future. The cost of staying in the same environment wasn't just my limitation; it was his inheritance.

At eighteen, a friend's father sat me down and taught me about credit, about building something from nothing, about thinking beyond the next meal to the next generation. At that same age, when most kids were thinking about prom and graduation parties, I was writing goals for my hair business, calculating exactly how many clients I needed to cover rent, buy clothing, and maybe, just maybe, something extra to save.

My mother's absence had hardened me, yes, but it had also taught me the most valuable lesson: Nobody was coming to save me. That sounds harsh, but it was the most liberating realization of my life. If nobody was coming to save me, then I was free to save myself. If nobody was going to hand me opportunities, then I was free to create them.

THE LEAP THAT CHANGES EVERYTHING

By twenty-one, I was back in New York, and I'd saved a couple of thousand dollars. This wasn't much by most standards, but a fortune for someone who'd started with nothing. New York was suffocating me. Everywhere I looked, I saw the same cycles repeating. Friends from high school were on their second or third child, still living in the same neighborhoods, still hoping for different results from the same choices.

"I'm moving to Georgia," I announced to anyone who would listen.

The response was universal disbelief. "Move to Georgia for what?" "What if it doesn't work out?" "That's crazy with a four-year-old." "You'll be back in a month."

Fear and faith cannot coexist. I'd learned that in the hardest possible way. Fear told me to stay where things were familiar, even if familiar meant limited. Faith told me to pack everything I owned into a U-Haul, strap my car to the back, and drive toward possibility with my son beside me.

The first month in Georgia, I cold-called salons from the Yellow Pages. I walked into shops with my portfolio and my story, asking for a chance. Fifteen salons said no. Some were polite about it. Others looked at me as a young, Black, single mother with no local references, and didn't even pretend to consider it.

Each "no" stung, but it also taught me something crucial: A "no" isn't final. It's just "not right now." It's information, not condemnation. It's redirection, not rejection. The sixteenth salon said yes, and that yes changed everything.

But here's what nobody tells you about breakthrough moments: They're expensive. Not in money, but in everything else. Moving to Georgia cost me my comfort zone, my familiar surroundings, and any safety net I might have had. Starting over cost me my pride. Do you know how humiliating it is to have people reject you fifteen times when you're trying to feed your child? Success would eventually cost me my marriage to someone who couldn't see my vision, relationships with people threatened by my growth, and the approval of those who preferred the old version of me.

THE COMPOUND INTEREST OF COURAGE

That salon in Georgia became my laboratory for learning that success isn't just about talent, it's about tenacity. Within six months, I'd built a clientele. Within three years, I was making as much money as my ex-husband, who'd told me to quit. Within five years, I owned my own salon. Each level of success brought new challenges, new costs, and new reasons to potentially quit.

When Gabriel was older, I'd take him with me to the salon. He'd do his homework in the back room while I worked. He watched me work fifteen-hour days, saw me handle difficult clients with grace, and witnessed me managing books until 2 a.m. He was learning by osmosis what I'd had to teach myself: Success isn't magic. It's showing up when you don't feel like it. It's doing the work when nobody's watching. It's betting on yourself when nobody else will.

The greatest tragedy happened when I lost Gabriel. He was my reason for everything, my motivation for every early morning and late night. The grief nearly destroyed me. Depression wrapped around me like chains. But even in that darkness, especially in that darkness, I learned the ultimate truth about the cost of not trying: It dishonors everything and everyone we've loved.

Years later, when I lost my father—the one man who believed in me, who opened my mind to a world bigger than my circumstances—I wanted to quit. The grief was suffocating. Then, waking up in a hospital bed after an accident, having doctors tell me I might lose my leg, I felt defeated. I was tired, and the physical pain was unbearable. But each time, I calculated the cost of quitting versus the cost of continuing, and the math always came out the same: I couldn't afford to stop.

THE INVOICE COMES DUE

Today, I'm a successful financial strategist. I help other entrepreneurs—many of them women who were told they couldn't, shouldn't, or wouldn't—build their dreams into reality, despite financial missteps or lack of financial literacy. When they come to me with their fears, their limitations, their carefully calculated reasons why they can't take the leap, I ask them one question:

"What's the cost of not trying?"

Because here's what I know after all these years, all these battles, all these losses and wins: The cost of not trying compounds over time. It's not just the business you don't start; it's the example you don't set. It's not just the money you don't make; it's the generational wealth you don't create. It's not just the dream you don't pursue; it's the permission you don't give others to pursue theirs.

Every time you choose not to try, you're writing a check against your future. Every time you let someone else's "no" become your stop sign, you're paying interest on their limitations. Every time you choose comfort over growth, familiarity over possibility, fear over faith, you're accumulating debt that your children and their children will have to pay.

But here's the beautiful flip side: Every time you try—even if you fail, especially if you fail—you're making deposits into your account of self-belief. Every risk you take teaches someone watching that risks are worth taking. Every time you get back up, you're showing someone else that falling isn't final.

Young, with a couple of thousand dollars, a four-year-old son, and determination, I wasn't just changing locations when I moved to Georgia. I was moving our entire lineage from one trajectory to another. When I kept calling salons after fifteen rejections, I wasn't just looking for a job. I was teaching my son that "no" is just part of the journey to "yes." When I built my business despite every statistic that said I couldn't, I wasn't just building income. I was building proof that statistics don't determine destiny.

YOUR INVOICE IS WAITING

Right now, you're standing at your own crossroads. Maybe it's not as dramatic as moving across the country with a child and no safety net. Maybe it's not as stark as choosing between survival and escape. But you're standing there, calculating the cost of trying versus the cost of staying exactly where you are.

Let me make this simple for you: The cost of not trying is everything.

It's the book you don't write that could have changed someone's life. It's the business you don't start that could have employed dozens. It's the conversation you don't have that could have healed a relationship. It's the example you don't set that could have inspired someone to change their entire trajectory.

You want to know what qualifies me to push you like this? I'm a teen mom who battled depression after losing her only child. I'm a daughter who buried the one man who truly loved her. I'm a woman who woke up in a hospital bed, being told she might lose her leg. And I'm still here, still building, still trying.

Not because I'm special. Not because I'm stronger than you. But because I've done the math, and the cost of not trying is a price I refuse to pay.

The question isn't whether you can afford to try. The question is whether you can afford not to. The invoice for playing small, for choosing safe, for listening to the chorus of "no" instead of finding your one "yes"—that invoice comes due eventually. And when it does, it charges interest on every dream deferred, every opportunity declined, every moment you chose fear over faith.

So, what's it going to be? You can keep calculating the reasons why not. You can keep listening to the people who made six hundred dollars look like failure instead of a starting point. You can keep choosing the familiar limitations over the unfamiliar possibilities.

Or you can do what I did in that moment when my ex-husband told me to quit: You can let their disbelief become your fuel. You can turn their "no" into your "watch me." You can decide that the cost of not trying is a debt you refuse to pass on to the next generation.

The choice is yours. The cost is clear. The only question left is: What are you willing to pay for the life you really want?

Because if a teen mom from the inner city who raised herself from age twelve can build success from scratch, if someone who buried their child and their father and almost lost their life and their leg can still keep fighting and winning—then what's your excuse?

What's the cost of not trying?

What if it doesn't work? But what if it does?

About Angel

Angel Spear is a financial strategist, educator, mentor, and legacy builder whose life's work is rooted in one unwavering belief: your past does not get to decide your future.

Her story did not begin in boardrooms or financial institutions, but in resilience. As a young woman navigating hardship, responsibility, and loss, Angel learned early that survival requires discipline—but thriving requires vision. By the age of twelve, Angel was already working—learning structure, service, and entrepreneurship through doing hair, a craft she would continue professionally for over two decades. From adolescence through age thirty-seven, she built clientele, income, and independence long before she ever learned the formal language of finance. Those years sharpened her ability to serve people where they were, listen beyond words, and create stability without a safety net.

In July of 2016, Angel's life shifted irrevocably with the loss of her son, Gabriel. Grief arrived without warning and with no instruction manual. The pain was paralyzing, and for a time, simply continuing felt impossible. Yet in the depth of that loss, Angel made a pivotal decision: she would not allow heartbreak to end her story. She turned grief into grit and decided that her story would not end in sorrow—but in significance.

Years later, in January of 2022, Angel suffered another devastating loss with the passing of her father—the man who had nurtured her imagination. His belief in possibility had fueled her long before success came into view, and his absence cemented her resolve to honor that legacy through intentional actions.

Today, Angel is widely known as The Finance Angel, a trusted financial strategist, educator, and mentor who guides individuals and entrepreneurs toward clarity, confidence, and control over their financial lives. She helps clients strategically leverage credit to access bank-backed capital for starting, growing, or scaling businesses, with a focused emphasis on protecting and building long-term wealth through life insurance. Through education and example, Angel demystifies money—transforming it from a source of fear and confusion into a tool for freedom and legacy.

Angel Spear continues to demonstrate that transformation does not require perfection, only willingness. Every room she enters, and every life she touches reflect her commitment to reminding us that purpose doesn't arrive after healing—it is often what carries us through it.

She is committed to reaching millions with practical tools, heartfelt truth, and strategies for generational wealth and impact.

Learn more at: ThefinanceAngel.com
Facebook and Instagram: @ThefinanceAngel

CHAPTER 21

FAILED AT GIVING UP: WHEN EVERYTHING MEANT TO BREAK ME BUILT MY EMPIRE

BY KEISHA ATLEE

By the time I got the call, my son was breathing fine. He was stable. But I was three hours away in Pennsylvania, phone pressed to my ear, feeling that jolt of panic the school nurse had planted with her alarming description of his condition. As he calmly explained from the emergency room what had happened, irritation rose alongside relief. Meanwhile, a teacher I'd never met sat beside him, ear hustling, taking notes. Notes that would become ammunition.

"I'm not turning around," I told him, keeping my voice steady even as my chest tightened. "Your dad and Grandpa are on their way." They were already en route—one just thirty minutes away, the other about an hour—because I'd prearranged for them to step in while I was traveling for work. And at home, my live-in nanny had the other kids covered as usual. Those eleven words would cost me two years of fighting child protective services, a lawyer I couldn't afford, and sleepless nights wondering if the system I'd devoted my career to would destroy me for being a Black single mother who dared to keep working.

The school nurse had already decided my story before I could tell it. Black mother. Four kids. A social worker who should "know better." Missing inhaler paperwork, but never mind that I'd been to the doctor three times trying to get it signed, that appointments kept getting cancelled, and that my son had his inhaler at home but needed special forms for school. Two days before summer break, his asthma flared because he'd been running around at recess. When I pushed back, knowing my rights and knowing the law, she found another way to punish me.

Child abandonment. Child neglect. The accusations landed like grenades in my professional life. As a licensed clinical social worker who'd spent years protecting children, I suddenly found myself on the other side of the system, fighting accusations that could end my career and destroy my business.

And it wasn't the first time.

The story really began years earlier, when I was pregnant with that same son, my eighteen-month-old daughter toddling around my legs. I did what I'd always done when life tried to bury me. I kept working. Through the pregnancy, through the fear, through the shame. I worked until the day I delivered my son, because I had a bigger goal: my clinical social work license. That piece of paper represented proof that my worst moments wouldn't define my destiny.

After giving birth, while other mothers were posting nursery photos, I was studying for the licensing exam, and after memorizing diagnostic criteria and treatment modalities. I passed on the first attempt.

But victory was temporary. The bankruptcy came next. It was the first of two that would mark my financial records like scarlet letters. I had moved back in with my parents, left the house, returned to it, lost it again, and eventually went through a short sale. Each move felt like a failure, but opportunities kept appearing. An amazing job would surface just when I needed it most. As I told people later, "Even through all my dumb decisions, God always had a hand on me."

The second bankruptcy hit in 2018, after my fourth child was born. I lost my car, was unemployed, filed to get the car back, found work, and started the exhausting cycle of rebuilding again. By any measure, I should have been finished. A single mother of four, two bankruptcies, the world had plenty of evidence to write me off. Instead, I launched my first business, Evolve.

Then came 2020, the year that changed everything through unbearable loss and impossible gain. My father passed away, removing another pillar of support. My mother had passed five years prior. But just before his death, a colleague mentioned a credit repair specialist who'd helped her buy a half-million-dollar house. "Give him twelve hundred dollars," the man told me. "I'll get you a car and a house."

I'd previously calculated it would take until 2026 to qualify for a mortgage after bankruptcy. He called me before my father's funeral: "You're ready to get your car." For the first time in my life, I walked into a dealership with preferred credit and walked out with a Ford Explorer. Two months later: "Are you ready to buy a house?"

Making seventy-six thousand a year as a single mother of four shouldn't have qualified me for a three-hundred-twenty-five-thousand-dollar mortgage. But I'd been relentless in ways that didn't show on applications. I'd picked up part-time work immediately. When stimulus checks arrived, instead of spending them on immediate needs, I saved every penny. By July 2020, I was a home-owner and six years ahead of my own timeline.

Real relentlessness isn't about reaching a destination, but instead about what you do when people keep trying to tear down what you've built.

The LinkedIn notifications started shortly after my professional victories became visible. Three to four people every week for five years now—former colleagues who'd tried to destroy me, administrators, all checking my profile, monitoring my progress.

My business partner's betrayal should have ended my entrepreneurial dreams. I'd tried to quit so many times that my persistence had become involuntary, like breathing.

But here's what they didn't know about Keisha Atlee: I had already failed at giving up so many times that persistence had become my superpower. I had learned to succeed without applause, to build without encouragement, to rise without permission.

I entered a women's entrepreneur program, received a stipend, relaunched Allied Practice Space LLC, quit my full-time job, and established Empowerment

Threads merchandise for allied health professionals. A year later, I started my private therapy practice. Now, the same people who'd tried to destroy me watch my success from a distance, walking past me at professional events like strangers.

The false CPS reports were meant to be the final blow. Two separate incidents, both rooted in racism and professional jealousy. The second happened after my son spent a summer with my sister, who is a licensed nurse who documented every medication. When he returned, his doctor lied to CPS, claiming he had bacteria in his lungs when it was just elevated IgE levels from allergies. She accused me of not giving him medication when he hadn't even been with me all summer.

The system I'd devoted my career to improving turned its machinery against me. They were so desperate to find something wrong that they cited the absence of an EpiPen at school for a shrimp allergy, even when his allergy testing wasn't current, no EpiPen had been prescribed, and the school didn't even serve shrimp.

Each accusation required lawyers, documentation, and time away from work. The investigations stayed in the system for five years, shadows following my professional reputation.

But I had receipts. Medical records. Prescriptions. Appointment histories. I had learned something crucial: document everything, because when you're a Black single mother succeeding against the odds, someone will always try to prove you don't deserve it.

Nothing was ever substantiated. But the trauma remained, the knowledge that my success threatened people enough to weaponize child protective services against me.

"You're always winning at losing," my sister used to say, and she was right. Every loss became a win eventually. Every setback revealed a strength.

The relapses into depression still come. Days when I lock myself in my room, crying to my therapist, "Why can't I just be like everybody else—oblivious and stupid without goals?" His response cut through the self-pity: "Are you telling me you're ungrateful to God for all the gifts He's given you?"

Because that's the trap of relentlessness—sometimes you want to quit so badly that continuing feels like punishment. But then a vision comes. Despite my protests of "God, no more visions," the inspiration arrives anyway. I write it down. I keep building.

My children's fathers promised to destroy me: "You're going down. You're gonna lose everything." They didn't understand that I'd already lost everything multiple times and learned that loss is just rearrangement for something better. What's meant for you is meant for you. People can delay it, complicate it, fight it, but they can't take it.

The business continues growing. From eight in the morning to eight-thirty at night, I provide therapy while mothering four children in the spaces between sessions. Every stream of income represents a door someone tried to close that I kicked open anyway.

The watchers are still watching. Every week, the LinkedIn notifications confirm it. They can't understand how someone who should be broken keeps building. They don't realize that when you've failed at giving up enough times, persistence becomes your default setting.

My best friend, an international psychologist, often says, "Girl, I don't know how you do it. You can't make this stuff up." She's right, but so is my refusal to quit. It's not me driving this persistence; it's something bigger, something that knew my purpose before others formed their opinions.

This is what I need you to know if you're standing at the edge of your own breakthrough moment: You're already all in this thing called life. As Jordan Peterson says, you might as well do whatever you want to do. As Alex Hormozi puts it, worst case scenario, you die—and you won't, but even if you did, you wouldn't care because you'd be dead.

The alternative to pushing forward is suffering in stillness. If you're going to struggle anyway, struggle forward. Their opinions don't pay your bills. Their permission isn't required for your purpose.

I've never needed positive feedback to persist. That's what bothers people most—when your motivation isn't external, they can't control it. When your vision comes from something bigger than their opinion, they can't kill it.

This isn't about them. It never was. This is about the four children watching me build an empire from ashes. This is about every client who sits in my therapy office needing to see proof that persistence pays off, even when no one's clapping.

The house I'm sitting in while writing this shouldn't exist. The business shouldn't be thriving. By every metric the world uses to measure success. I should be a statistic, not a success story. But relentlessness doesn't care about metrics. It only cares about the next step, the next day, the next opportunity to prove that what's meant for you will find you.

Every attempt to destroy me just adds another chapter to my story of relentless resurrection. I'm not unbothered, I'm just no longer auditioning. Once you've survived your own undoing and stayed curious, threats start to lose their teeth. The grief is in the room—but it doesn't direct the dance. I've tried to quit. Truly. I've laid it down more times than I can count—convinced I was done. But every time I walk away, something taps my shoulder. A whisper, a vision, a thread I didn't know I was still holding. Turns out, failing to give up might be the greatest success of my life. I've collapsed into the silence of giving up, and still—something keeps breathing me back to the work. Not because I'm strong. Because the work remembers me, the dreams return uninvited. Each time I turn away, a new thread appears. A glimpse of what's possible. A tug from the future.

Just do it. Whatever that thing is that keeps calling you despite the bankruptcies, the betrayals, the deaths, the accusations—just do it. Not because it will be easy, not because anyone will understand. Do it because the vision won't leave you alone. Do it because you've already survived everything meant to destroy you.

This is about you finally understanding that failing at giving up might be the greatest success of your life.

About Keisha

Keisha Atlee, LCSW-C, writes from lived experience at the intersection of loss, purpose, and unwavering resolve. A licensed clinical social worker, entrepreneur, and mother of four, she has spent her career walking alongside people during their most vulnerable moments—knowing that strength is built in the ordinary and tested in the unexpected—and helping them rebuild when life refuses to follow the plan.

As the founder of Allied Practice Space, LLC, Keisha is committed to creating environments—both physical and internal—where people can do meaningful work and reclaim their sense of agency. Through her clinical practice, training work, and writing, she empowers others to confront what hurts, honor what matters, and move forward with conviction.

Known for blending clinical insight with real-world wisdom, she challenges the idea that resilience is about endurance alone. Instead, her work highlights clarity, self-trust, and the courage to keep choosing growth after disappointment, loss, or detour. Her work is grounded in the belief that healing is rarely linear and resilience is often quiet, persistent, and deeply personal. *Relentless* is an extension of that truth—a reminder that forward movement doesn't always roar; sometimes it simply refuses to stop.

Beyond her work, she finds restoration in tropical sunlight and the quiet company of a good book.

CHAPTER 22

CLAIM YOUR SEAT AT THE TABLE

BY NICK NANTON

I remember the exact moment I almost gave up. I had just lost the Emmy for my documentary. People say the right things in those moments. *It's an honor just to be nominated. You should be proud. Next time.*

And I nodded, smiled, said "thank you," and even believed some of it. I had poured my heart into that film, and the loss hit hard. For a moment…just a moment…I considered walking away from it all. It sounds melodramatic, and I do have to admit, it was my first documentary I'd ever made. But I had put a lot of time and effort into orchestrating my best effort, and had made it through to getting a nomination with my first try. I figured I must have done something right! The content was so heartfelt that in the moment I felt like if that couldn't win, it must be impossible to win!

That's the part we often edit out of the story. We like to pretend resilience is automatic. That relentless people never consider stopping. But the truth is, there are moments when continuing feels heavier than quitting. Moments when discouragement whispers, with precision, into the one place it knows you're vulnerable.

I did go on to win for directing the same film that night, and that was completely unexpected after losing for the film. But it was rocket fuel that propelled me onto the next project. I kept making films and, to date, have been honored with more than 20 Emmy Awards.

That night taught me something I've never forgotten: you cannot win a race you don't enter. And you cannot be considered for a life you opt out of.

Relentlessness isn't loud. Often, it shows up as a private decision to stay in the game when no one would blame you for walking away. For a long time, like most people who have graduated from school and sports, I won nothing. No awards. No external validation. There were years of real work in multiple fields, real sacrifice, and no trophies or accolades to show for it.

What most people don't realize—and what I didn't fully understand at first—is that awards don't just reward excellence. They reward *your willingness to compete*. You have to enter. And not casually. Not once. Not only in the category that feels safest. You have to enter intentionally and advocate for yourself and your project. You have to enter multiple categories where your work legitimately qualifies. Most people never do this. They assume someone else will notice and that recognition finds talent automatically. They think there's some invisible committee scanning the world for deserving work. There isn't. Awards don't hunt you down. You raise your hand. That first loss stung more than I expected. I told myself I was grateful and that it was progress. But inside, I was doing the quiet math every creator does in moments like that: *Is this worth continuing?*

Years later, when the recognition became consistent, the feeling wasn't explosive. It was steady. Confirming. Relentless people don't wait to feel confident. They choose to stay *eligible.*

* * *

Probably the most intimidating part of my work is asking for time with some of the most famous people in the world. I always ask carefully and respectfully and follow the unspoken etiquette of the industry. If I want to connect with someone, I know the process: I have to ask the intermediary, then they ask the person, and then I wait. Sometimes for years.

One day, I realized I was in a room I didn't have to negotiate my way into. I was working on the *Dickie V* documentary and met some extraordinary people. One day, my phone pinged, and it was a group text. Names appeared on my phone that had once felt untouchable. Shaquille O'Neal and Charles Barkley were in that group chat, and someone thought I should be a part of it. But here's something no one prepares you for: that moment can be deeply uncomfortable. Not because of ego, but because of identity.

I don't hate the phrase *imposter syndrome*, but I think it's misunderstood. If you never feel that tension, you're probably not stretching. Growth *should* feel destabilizing. If you look back on your earlier work and don't cringe a little, you might not be evolving. For a moment, I hesitated to respond to the group text. My inner monologue challenged me, wondering if anyone cared what I had to say. I had to remind myself that I had done the work to get there. I had made those connections honestly and respectfully. What I was really learning was how to belong without shrinking.

There's a version of humility that's actually fear in disguise. It sounds like gratitude, but it's rooted in the hope that if you downplay yourself enough, no one will notice you're still a little scared and take the invitation back. True humility doesn't deny the work. It acknowledges it and then places it in context. Maya Angelou once said something profound about success. That no matter how far you go, there's always a voice that whispers, *they're going to find out*. Find out you don't belong. Find out you're not as good as they think. Find out you slipped in through a side door. The irony is that the voice often still shows up after you've earned the seat.

The lesson wasn't to silence that voice with bravado. It was to answer it with truth. I belong here not because I'm perfect but because I showed up, stayed in the game, honored the process, and didn't leave when it got uncomfortable.

Humility, I've learned, isn't pretending you don't belong. It's standing fully where you are, grateful for the hands that lifted you, honest about the effort it took, and secure enough not to apologize for the space you now occupy. That's not arrogance. That's integrity. And it's one of the quiet disciplines of being relentless.

THE POINT OF VIEW I DIDN'T KNOW I HAD

I've been making films for years now, but I consider myself a lifelong student, and I am always open to feedback. Over time, I noticed I kept getting the same advice over and over: *to be a great director, you need a point of view.* That advice confused me. I just wanted to tell stories. Recently, though, an idea took hold that would bring this lesson home.

My daughter, Addison, is a dancer and has acro in her dances. Acro is gymnastics tricks woven into dance. Her coach, Scott Johnson, was on the 1984 Olympic gymnastics team and won the gold medal. He is a man who achieved something extraordinary, and yet people don't stop him in the grocery store. He isn't recognized on the street. That contrast stuck with me.

As I researched, layers of a story emerged. The 1980 Olympics were boycotted by the United States. Three men on Scott's team never got to compete. Then, in 1984, Russia boycotted the Los Angeles Games. Cold War politics led to athletes making sacrifices. Now, the Summer Olympics are returning to LA in 2028, and here we are, back in a tense relationship with Russia. I started to wonder if there was a deeper human story there. I wondered if I could somehow learn geopolitics through the lens of these gymnastics teams and share that knowledge with the world. What does grit look like when history intervenes? What does perseverance mean when opportunity disappears through no fault of your own?

I mentioned the idea to my team. No one seemed excited. So, I dug deeper. I stopped telling them about my idea and started showing. I painted the vision cinematically, outlining the pacing, the emotional arc, the deeper meaning beneath the sport. Suddenly, they got it. They not only got it, they were excited to see if we could make it a reality. So, I got to work, and within weeks, contracts were signed to make a film. That's when I understood. That was the point of view. It's not an opinion, but a vision others couldn't yet see. I was given the vision and therefore carried a responsibility. If a vision is given to you, you can't expect others to understand what was entrusted to you alone. You have to share it in a way that they can see it and get as excited about it as you are.

Being relentless isn't just about execution. It's about staying loyal to the idea long enough for it to fully reveal itself. Most ideas don't arrive complete. They come as fragments, an image, a tension, a question you can't shake. When you first share them, they're often received as half-formed or impractical, not because they lack value, but because they haven't yet been translated into something others can see. That's where most people stop. They confuse a lack of immediate enthusiasm with a lack of merit. Relentlessness means you don't abandon the idea at that stage. You refine it. You give it shape, language, and form. You stay with it until it becomes undeniable. Sometimes this takes years, trust me! I couldn't expect my team to be excited about a vision I hadn't fully honored myself. Once I committed to carrying it all the way from intuition to articulation, the response changed; not because the idea was suddenly better, but because it was finally clear.

Purpose works the same way. It isn't validated by consensus. It's clarified through commitment. Relentlessness, I've learned, is the discipline of saying yes to the responsibility that comes with insight. It's the willingness to stand by an idea before it's understood.

The same lesson showed up again during the production of *Dickie V*. ESPN wasn't interested at first. So, I raised the money myself. I executed the vision anyway. Once they saw the whole thing come to fruition, they wanted it. This is not a dig at ESPN. To be fair, I hadn't sold my vision well enough at the start to help them see the value in it. I had to execute on it in order to show what was in my head. That pattern has repeated itself more times than I can count. Vision first. Execution second. Validation last, if it comes at all.

What idea keeps returning to you, even when you try to move on to something easier or more accepted? What might change if you stopped waiting for enthusiasm and committed instead to *clarity*? Where in your life are you being invited to stay with an idea longer, not to prove it, but to steward it? Your point of view doesn't need consensus. It needs commitment and the courage to carry it until it can stand on its own.

BEING UNDERESTIMATED— AND LETTING THE WORK RESPOND

One of the more predictable parts of choosing an unconventional path is being misunderstood along the way. I had worked for months to secure a meeting with an iconic media personality. Later, I learned that his agent had warned him against working with me. I found out that he had said, "This guy seems like a fast talker. I don't think you should do this." I wasn't offended. I understood it. In this industry, confidence without a familiar résumé can sound like inflated noise. Luckily, the celebrity worked with me anyway, and a year later, that same agent admitted that he hadn't thought I could pull it off. That moment wasn't satisfying in the way you'd imagine. It wasn't about proving someone wrong. It was confirmation of something I've come to rely on: the work speaks far more clearly than persuasion ever could.

Broadway would bring another round of skepticism. It started the way many big ideas do, half-formed and vulnerable to logistics. I met with an agent who told me that his client was ready for a global stage. I knew if I could produce a Broadway show for her, she would get the kind of recognition they were looking for. We scheduled meetings. Flights were booked. Then, one by one, the meetings disappeared. Calendars collapsed. Plans unraveled. Industry veterans questioned my every move. But I knew that a Broadway show was the game-changer she needed, and I wasn't going to give up.

Months later, when I called the agent and told him it was happening, there was silence on the line. Then disbelief. She performed a near sell-out show and to rave reviews. Relentlessness isn't about insisting you're right. It's a willingness to walk down every possible avenue to get the result you want.

If I know something is *technically* possible, I don't treat it as a stretch. I treat it as a problem to be solved. Maybe the traditional funding method won't work. Maybe execution needs to look different. Maybe the team needs to expand. I pivot and experiment until I get results. And I don't do it alone. I partner with people who are exceptional at things I struggle with. I build teams of people who are smarter and more talented than me in their domains. I let them do what they do best while I hold the vision steady.

Relentlessness isn't ego. It's orchestration. It's the relentless pursuit of a favorable outcome. Stubbornness clings to being right; relentlessness stays devoted to the *result*, no matter how many times the path has to change.

* * *

Looking back, I can see that none of these moments were isolated. The night I almost stopped competing, the ideas that wouldn't let me go, the projects people doubted, they were all teaching me the same lesson from different angles.

Relentlessness isn't about refusing to quit out of pride. It's about refusing to abandon what you've been entrusted with. You enter again because the work deserves another chance. You stay in the room because you've earned the right to be there. You keep shaping the idea because it was given to *you* to carry. You let the work speak because you understand persuasion is temporary, but execution endures.

For a long time, I thought relentlessness meant pushing harder, faster, louder. I know now it's quieter than that. More disciplined. More reverent. Relentlessness is the choice to remain available to the vision even when validation is delayed. To stand fully in your place without shrinking, to stay with an idea long enough for it to become clear, and to answer doubt not with defensiveness but with hard work.

There will always be reasons to stop entering, to step out of the room, to wait until you feel more ready. But confidence is not the prerequisite. Commitment is. You don't become relentless by never questioning yourself. You become relentless by deciding, again and again, that the calling is worth the discomfort. So, you raise your hand. You take the meeting. You refine the idea. You assemble the right people. And you *stay.* Not because it's easy or guaranteed. But because the life you're meant to live requires it.

About Nick

From the slums of Port-au-Prince, Haiti, with special forces raiding a sex trafficking ring and freeing children, to the Virgin Galactic Space Port in Mojave with Sir Richard Branson, twenty-two-time Emmy Award–winning Director-Producer Nick Nanton has become known for telling stories that connect. Why? Because he focuses on the most fascinating subject in the world: *people.* As an award-winning songwriter, storyteller, and best-selling author, Nick has shared his message with millions of people through his documentaries, speeches, blogs, lectures, songs, and best-selling books. Nick's book *StorySelling* hit The Wall Street Journal Best-Seller List and is available on Audible as an audiobook. Nick has directed more than sixty documentaries and a sold-out Broadway Show (garnering forty-three Emmy nominations in multiple regions and twenty-two wins), including:

- *DICKIE V* (ESPN/Disney+)
- *Rudy Ruettiger: The Walk On* (Amazon Prime)
- *The Rebound* (Netflix)
- *Operation Toussaint* (Amazon Prime)

Nick has shared the stage with, coauthored books with, and made films featuring:

- Larry King
- Kathie Lee Gifford
- Hoda Kotb
- Dick Vitale
- Kenny Chesney
- Magic Johnson
- Coach Mike Krzyzewski
- Jack Nicklaus
- Tony Robbins
- Lisa Nichols
- Peter Diamandis
- And many more

Nick specializes in bringing the element of human connection to every viewer, no matter the subject. He is currently directing and hosting the series *In Case You Didn't Know* (season 1 executive produced by Larry King), featuring legends in the worlds of business, entrepreneurship, personal development, technology, and sports.

Nick's first love has always been music. He has been writing songs for more than two decades, and his songs have been aired on radio across the United States and in Canada. He is currently ranked in the top 10 percent of songwriters in the world. His songs have been recorded by Lee Brice, Darius Rucker, RaeLynn, Joe Bryson, and many more, and have amassed more than three million streams on Spotify, Apple Music, Pandora, and SoundCloud. He received three Gold records in 2018 for his work with the global touring band A Day to Remember.

Nick has written and/or produced songs that have appeared on the following shows or in promotional commercials for:

- the Fox prime-time series *Glee, New Girl, House*, and *Hell's Kitchen*
- the MLB All-Star Game
- ABC Family's hit series *Falcon Beach*
- the CBS prime-time series *Ghost Whisperer* starring Jennifer Love Hewitt

CHAPTER 23

FROM SURVIVAL MODE TO CEO MODE: BREAKING EVERY CYCLE THAT TRIED TO BREAK ME

BY KEISHA BURTON

The crack pipe sat on my uncle's kitchen table like a twisted invitation to surrender.

"Just hit it once," he said, his eyes glazed with the familiar haze I'd seen destroy so many in Pine Bluff. "It'll take all your problems away."

I was twenty-one, exhausted, with a baby on my hip and textbooks scattered across my apartment floor. Finals were in three days. My bank account showed $47. The eviction notice was two weeks old. Everyone I knew had already placed their bets on when I'd drop out—not if, but when.

My uncle pushed the pipe closer. "You're trying too hard, baby girl. This is easier."

That moment crystallized everything. I looked at my daughter, Alise, sleeping in my arms, then back at him. This man I loved was offering me the same escape route that had swallowed our entire neighborhood. In that instant, I understood the real choice wasn't between staying in school or dropping out. It was between becoming another cautionary tale or becoming the woman who refused to let statistics write her story.

"No," I said, standing up with my baby pressed against my chest. "That's not my story."

I walked out of his house and never went back. That night, I studied until 4 a.m. with my daughter sleeping beside me, the weight of generations pressing down on my shoulders. But pressure, I was learning, could either crush you or forge you into something unbreakable.

Pine Bluff, Arkansas, isn't where dreams go to thrive; it's where they go to die quietly. The crime rate is suffocating. Poverty is generational. The expectation is survival, not success. My paternal grandmother, Cora, only had an eighth-grade education. When her military husband died, leaving her with nine children and no benefits, she did what she had to do to survive. Then her sister was murdered in cold blood, and Cora took in two more children without hesitation.

When one of her sons had a child with a woman who felt she couldn't raise the baby, that woman showed up at my grandmother Cora's house and left the child in her care. And as she had done so many times before, Cora didn't hesitate. She took that baby in, too—no questions asked, no judgment, just pure responsibility and love.

Twelve mouths to feed. No education. No child support. No government assistance that actually helped. No way out except through.

I grew up watching the women in my family survive but never thrive. They stayed in bad relationships because they couldn't afford to leave. They endured abuse because a bad man with a paycheck seemed better than no man and no money. They worked multiple minimum-wage jobs that barely covered rent, let alone dreams. They aged decades in years, their potential buried under the crushing weight of just getting by.

My mother had me young, too young to know better, old enough to know life had just gotten infinitely harder. My father?

My father wasn't a bad man, and he wasn't on drugs—he just had different priorities. Sometimes he was more focused on hanging out with his friends or being around women, and as a child, that meant he wasn't always as present as I needed him to be. But he still showed up at different points in my life.

I'll never forget when I told him in my junior year that I was on track to graduate. He didn't discourage me, but he did ask a question that stuck with me: "How long is that going to last?" Not out of malice, but out of the mindset he'd grown up with—a mindset shaped by generations of instability and low expectations. It wasn't personal. It was cultural. It was familiar. But to me, it became fuel.

But something in me refused to accept that narrative. Maybe it was teenage rebellion. Maybe it was divine intervention. Maybe it was just pure, stubborn refusal to let my story end where theirs began. When I got accepted to the University of Arkansas at Pine Bluff, I was the first in my family to step foot on a college campus as a student, not as a janitor or cafeteria staff member. No blueprint. No mentor. No money. No one to call when I didn't understand financial aid forms or how to register for classes. Just determination and a library card I'd gotten at twelve because books were free entertainment.

Then, freshman year, I got pregnant. The father disappeared faster than morning mist. My mother's solution was simple:

My mother had me young, and she knew firsthand how hard it was to raise a child without support. When I got pregnant in college, her advice wasn't cruel—it was practical. "Maybe you should quit school and get a full-time job," she said. Not because she didn't believe in me, but because she wanted me to have stability, something she never had enough of. She didn't tell me to go work at a plant or follow the path of my grandmother. She just wanted to make sure I could take care of my baby. But deep down, I knew quitting school would only repeat the same cycle I was trying so hard to break.

But I'd already seen where that road led. I'd watched too many brilliant women in my family trade their potential for a paycheck that never quite covered the bills, for men who never quite treated them right, for dreams that never quite had space to breathe. So I did something that nobody in my family had ever done before. I stayed in school.

I became a master of impossible juggling acts. Class from 8 a.m. to noon. Work study job from 1 p.m. to 5 p.m. Back to campus for night classes. I studied from 10 p.m. to 2 a.m. while my daughter slept beside me in the single bed in my dorm room. I woke up at 5 a.m. when she cried. Change her, feed her, rock her back to sleep. Grab two hours of sleep before it all started again. Repeat. Survive. Persist.

The exhaustion was bone-deep, soul-deep, the kind that makes you hallucinate during lectures. There were nights I fell asleep over my textbooks, waking up to baby formula spilled across my economics homework, the equations blurred beyond recognition. I had to redo that assignment three times. I sold Mary Kay on weekends to anyone who would listen to my pitch, did hair in my dorm room bathroom for $20 a head, and typed papers with one hand while bottle-feeding with the other. I learned to study with Barney singing in the background, to write essays while bouncing a crying baby, to take phone interviews for internships while hiding in the dormitory stairwell so no one would hear her babbling.

I joined the investment club on campus, and because I attended an HBCU, I wasn't the only Black woman in the room—far from it. What I was, however, was a young mother trying to build a different future, sitting beside peers who didn't have the same responsibilities waiting for them at home.

When the club planned a trip to New York to visit Wall Street, I couldn't afford it at first. But our professors believed in exposing us to bigger possibilities. They rallied sponsors to cover the cost, and because of them, I went. That trip changed everything. Seeing the New York Stock Exchange in person opened my eyes to a level of wealth and opportunity I didn't even know existed. It planted seeds in my spirit that I couldn't un-see, couldn't un-dream.

The financial aid office became my second home. I learned to navigate bureaucracy like a pro, filling out form after form, appeal after appeal. When they said I didn't qualify for certain grants, I researched others. When those fell through, I found scholarships nobody was applying for—$500 here for an essay about overcoming adversity (I had plenty of material), $300 there for students who were parents, $250 for first-generation college students. I applied for everything, even scholarships for left-handed people (I'm right-handed, but desperate times called for creative applications).

My GPA wasn't perfect. How could it be? But every semester I survived felt like a victory against impossible odds. Every exam I passed while my daughter had a fever was a small revolution. Every presentation I delivered on three hours of sleep was proof that my father was wrong, that my uncles were wrong, that everyone who bet against me had underestimated what a desperate woman with a dream could accomplish. My GPA started off rocky—balancing motherhood, classes, and survival will do that. But once I found my rhythm, something shifted. I tightened my focus, got organized, asked for help when I needed it, and worked like a woman determined to change her entire bloodline. By the time I graduated, not only had I survived everything thrown at me, I also finished with over a 3.0 GPA. That degree wasn't just a piece of paper; it was proof of discipline, resilience, and God's grace over my life.

The isolation was suffocating. While other students were at parties, I was reading "Goodnight Moon" for the hundredth time. While they stressed about spring break plans to Cancun, I stressed about whether the electricity would stay on through winter. I became an expert at making $20 worth of groceries last two weeks, at finding free campus events that provided food, and at studying in buildings that stayed open late so I could use their heat and electricity instead of my own. I knew which vending machines sometimes gave two snacks for the price of one, which professors kept snacks in their offices for hungry students, and which churches near campus served free dinners on Wednesday nights.

Then there was the shame—the hot, suffocating shame of being different. I brought my daughter to campus when the babysitter fell through, trying to keep her quiet in the back of lecture halls. Of wearing the same three outfits on rotation because formula and diapers came before fashion. I didn't get to live the typical college social life, but I wasn't completely isolated either. I had help—real help—from my grandmother, my mother, and a few close friends who stepped in when I needed a moment to breathe. I still had fun sometimes. I still went out occasionally. I laughed, took breaks, lived life. It wasn't all struggle. But even in those moments, responsibility was always waiting for me when I got back. I watched other girls my age worry about their nail appointments while I worried about having enough gas to get to campus.

But I kept going. My family never asked why I was trying to be better than them—they wanted the best for me. But they did wonder why I made things so hard on myself. "Why are you doing so much?" "Why don't you slow down?" "Why are you stressing yourself out like this?" They weren't criticizing me;

they just didn't understand the pressure I felt to rewrite our story. They didn't yet see that my "doing too much" was exactly what it was going to take to break generational cycles. Even when professors suggested I take a semester off, "given your circumstances." Even when my daughter got sick, I had to choose between missing an exam and leaving her with someone I didn't trust. I chose the exam and cried the entire time I was taking it, my tears blurring the Scantron bubbles.

The shift happened gradually, then suddenly. Junior year, something clicked. I stopped apologizing for my presence in rooms where I was the only one who looked like me. I stopped explaining why I was "still trying" to finish school. I stopped believing that struggle was my permanent address. I realized every obstacle I overcame was building a strength that my classmates with trust funds would never have.

I discovered that the business education I was fighting so hard for wasn't just about getting a degree; it was about learning a language that had been kept from my family for generations. The language of equity. Of compound interest. Of investment strategies. Of generational wealth building. Every class was filling in gaps that poverty had created, teaching me things that wealthy families discussed over dinner tables while mine discussed which utility to pay first.

I became obsessed with certifications and licenses. Real estate. Life insurance. Securities. Each license was another key to doors that had been locked to people like me. I was arming myself for a revolution—a quiet, personal revolution against every limitation that had been placed on me since birth.

When I walked across that graduation stage, my daughter on my hip and my MBA in hand, I wasn't just the first in my family to graduate from college. I was proof that cycles could be broken and that statistics were just numbers, not prophecies.

Today, I'm a CEO, real estate broker, life insurance broker, mentor, and a mother. But more than any title, I'm a translator. I translate the language of success for people who were never taught to speak it.

Here's what breaking generational cycles actually requires:

You have to become comfortable being uncomfortable. Every room you're *not supposed* to be in? That's exactly where you need to be. The discomfort you feel is growth happening in real-time.

You have to learn to monetize your story, not romanticize your struggle. Your mess becomes your message, but only if you do the work to extract the lessons and teach others.

You have to build while you heal. You don't get to wait until you're *ready*, *whole*, or *qualified*. You build with broken pieces until they become a masterpiece.

You have to stop asking for permission to be excellent. Nobody is going to hand you a certificate that says you're worthy of success. You have to decide you are, then move accordingly.

I spend weekends teaching community seminars, breaking down financial concepts into language my community understands. I mentor a young girl through Big Brothers Big Sisters, who reminds me of myself, all fire and fight, but aimed in the wrong direction. I tell her what I wish someone had told me: "Channel that energy into business, baby. Fighting the world won't change it, but building something will."

You don't need anyone's permission to be relentless. You need three things: faith, focus, and a refusal to let your current situation write your final chapter.

My grandmother, Cora, raised twelve children with an eighth-grade education. I'm raising the next generation of my family with an MBA and a real estate empire. The gap between where you are and where you want to be isn't talent, connections, or timing. It's tenacity. Your next decision can change everything.

Be relentless. Your family's future is counting on it.

About Keisha

Keisha Burton is a dynamic entrepreneur, real estate broker, life insurance broker, speaker, author, and the visionary CEO of 7Nine Consulting LLC. Known for her unstoppable determination and heart-centered leadership, she embodies what it means to be *Relentless*, turning every obstacle into an opportunity and every challenge into a stepping stone toward generational transformation.

Born and raised in Pine Bluff, Arkansas, Keisha became the first in her family to graduate from college, earning her Bachelor's degree in Business Management from the University of Arkansas at Pine Bluff and later her MBA from Webster University. Her journey from young mother navigating college life to multi-licensed financial and real estate professional reflects her belief that your starting point does not define your finish line.

Keisha's early career began in auditing and accounting before she transitioned into sales, ultimately discovering her passion for real estate and financial empowerment. Today, she serves as a licensed Real Estate Broker and Life Insurance Broker, using her expertise to help families build wealth through property ownership, strategic life insurance planning, and financial education. She is known for simplifying complex concepts and giving her clients the tools and confidence to build a lasting legacy.

A devoted mother and proud GiGi, Keisha centers her life around faith, family, service, and impact. She mentors young women, teaches community financial-literacy seminars, partners with local organizations, and inspires others through her transparency, resilience, and lived wisdom.

As a co-author in a national book project with world-renowned motivational icon Les Brown, Keisha shares elements of her personal journey—Breaking The Cycle: From Bills to Blessings—offering readers practical wisdom, heartfelt encouragement, and the unshakable reminder that being *Relentless* is not just a personality trait, but a decision to rise no matter what tries to break you.

Keisha continues to expand her legacy by helping others build theirs. Her mission is clear: educate, elevate, and equip individuals to create the life they deserve—one courageous decision, one strategy, and one breakthrough at a time.

www.ingramcontent.com/pod-product-compliance
Ingram Content Group UK Ltd.
Pitfield, Milton Keynes, MK11 3LW, UK
UKHW021523300726
14060UKWH00017B/750/J